UKRAINE UNBROKEN

ALWAYS

Jonathan Myerson

FIVE DAY WAR

David Edgar

THREE MATES

Natalka Vorozhbyt
translated by Sasha Dugdale

WRETCHED THINGS

David Greig

TAKEN

Cat Goscovitch

UKRAINE UNBROKEN

Five Plays by

Jonathan Myerson
David Edgar
Natalka Vorozhbyt
translated by Sasha Dugdale
David Greig
Cat Goscovitch

NICK HERN BOOKS

London
www.nickhernbooks.co.uk

A Nick Hern Book

Ukraine Unbroken first published in Great Britain in 2026 as a paperback original by Nick Hern Books Limited, The Glasshouse, 49a Goldhawk Road, London W12 8QP

Cover image: Bob King Creative

Designed and typeset by Nick Hern Books, London
Printed in the UK by Mimeo Ltd, Huntingdon, Cambridgeshire PE29 6XX

A CIP catalogue record for this book is available from the British Library

ISBN 978 1 83904 563 9

www.nickhernbooks.co.uk/environmental-policy

Nick Hern Books' authorised representative in the EU is
Easy Access System Europe – Mustamäe tee 50, 10621 Tallinn, Estonia
email gpsr.requests@easproject.com

Contents

Foreword
Nicolas Kent

Nearly twenty years ago, when British troops were fighting in Afghanistan, I had the idea of producing a trilogy of twelve half-hour plays outlining the history of Afghanistan since colonial days. That work, *The Great Game: Afghanistan*, came about mainly because, although there were British troops fighting in Helmand, I discovered while talking to many people there was almost no knowledge of Afghanistan's colonial past, its history or even that there had been previous Anglo-Afghan Wars – one of which resulted in the most comprehensive defeat ever of the British Army.

The public really engaged with this trilogy, and we played it twice at the Tricycle Theatre in London, and subsequently on a tour of four major cities in the United States including New York. Finally, a year later in 2011, through a joint initiative with the British Council, the Pentagon and the UK Ambassador to the US, we were invited back to Washington to present the plays over two days to an audience of 1500 USAID and Pentagon personnel.

About a decade later, after the second Russian invasion of Ukraine, I found that there was a similar ignorance about the history of Ukraine, and more particularly about what had happened in Ukraine since the dissolution of the Soviet Union. Almost no one I spoke to seemed to know much about the Budapest Memorandum of 1994 and its formal security guarantees from Russia, China, France, the USA and the UK for Ukraine's territorial integrity. Most people seem to be very hazy about the causes of the Maidan demonstrations of 2004 and 2014 and even fewer people – especially among the younger generation – seemed conscious of the fact that, despite the valiant efforts of some journalists to cast more light on this issue, in the last four years over 20,000 Ukrainian children have been abducted by the Russians and placed in schools in Russia for later adoption.

During these conversations in early 2025, the idea of doing something theatrically similar to the Afghan trilogy but about Ukraine began to germinate. I contacted a number of playwrights and particularly discussed the idea with David Edgar, David Greig and Cat Goscovitch, all of whom were very encouraging, and wanted to be part of it. However, given the steep decline in subsidy for the arts over the last two decades, a day-long trilogy on a subject like this was a daunting prospect.

Nevertheless, I pressed on with the idea, and during a lunch with an arts/education philanthropist, an expert on Eastern European politics, we discussed the idea and he asked to read the Afghan plays. A week later came the clincher: he wrote me a very enthusiastic email and made a very generous offer of seed money from which this whole larger project has grown. However, rather than a trilogy it has emerged as just one evening of five plays. This production became a reality when the wonderful Arcola Theatre, which has always been a home-from-home to me, expressed faith in the project on the basis of the first two scripts they were shown, and embraced it with enthusiasm.

I must thank so many people – Ukrainian, European, American and British – who have so generously helped fund this project and worked on it tirelessly to make it happen.

I hope that those seeing or reading these plays will understand this tragic conflict better, and that this theatrical venture can teach us something of the history of Ukraine and help us to empathise with the suffering this war is causing for so many millions of people.

February 2026

Ukraine Unbroken was first performed at Arcola Theatre, London, on 27 February 2026. The cast was as follows:

Daniel Betts
Ian Bonar
Sally Giles
David Michaels
Clara Read
Jade Williams

Bandura Player	Mariia Petrovska
Director	Nicolas Kent
Associate Director	Victoria Gartner
Set and Costume Designer	Michael Taylor
Lighting Designer	Matt Eagland
Sound and Video Designer	Joe Dines
Production Manager	Joe Prentice
Costume Supervisor	Alexa Moore
Stage Manager on Book	Naomi Shanson
Assistant Stage Manager	Ryan Denton
Casting Director	Nadine Rennie CDG
Assistant Director	Maryna Kursik
Story Support for Mariia Petrovska	John Farndon
Assistant to the Designer	Rebecca Ward
Stage Crew	Patrick Momodu-Akinola

This text went to press before the end of rehearsals and so may differ slightly from the plays as performed.

ALWAYS

Jonathan Myerson

Characters

SOFIYA
PETRO
JAROMIR
SNIPER

Hotel Ukraina, Maidan Nezalezhnosti, Kyiv, Thursday 20 February 2014, about 8 a.m.

A hotel bedroom, decorated in best Soviet style. The sun is rising through threadbare curtains.

SOFIYA stands in the middle of the room, using the hotel landline.

SOFIYA. Come on. Please.

> *She waits, listens to the ringtone at the other end.*

Please, please. Pick up. Come on.

> *She waits again.*

Come on! I. Just. Want. A – Please!

> *At which point PETRO re-enters the room. He is holding his mobile.*

> *He is surprised to see her awake and on the phone.*

PETRO. Who are you…?

> *SOFIYA slams the phone down.*

SOFIYA. I want a cup of coffee. Don't you?

PETRO. I can go down.

SOFIYA (*angry*). What the hell's room service for? Where are they all?

PETRO. I'll go down.

SOFIYA. Who were you talking to? Out there.

PETRO. No one.

SOFIYA. Your phone rang, you were out of here. That's a pretty big no one.

PETRO. Party business, that sort of thing.

He is getting dressed during this.

But she can see he is distracted.

SOFIYA. You don't usually – Tell me. What's the big secret?

PETRO. Don't ask. Please.

SOFIYA. Have they found out about Alex?

PETRO. No, no, thank God, not that.

SOFIYA. What then? You're being – it's something.

PETRO (*dialling his phone*). I need to talk to him. Is that alright? If I just talk to Alex?

SOFIYA. He'll be asleep.

PETRO. The whole place is up and awake. Sofiya. For God's sake, look!

SOFIYA *goes to the window, looks down:*

SOFIYA. What's going on? Something's happening.

PETRO. Something's going to happen.

SOFIYA. What? (*Urgent.*) That's what the call was about?

A moment. He doesn't deny it.

He gives up on ringing Alex, switches his phone off.

PETRO. His phone's off.

SOFIYA. It isn't. He never turns it off.

PETRO (*tensing up*). I can't get him to reply.

SOFIYA. Text him then. What is going to happen?

PETRO. Things.

SOFIYA. For God's sake, Petro, what?

PETRO. I can't tell you.

SOFIYA. Oh God. You never used to –

PETRO. I have a role now, obligations.

SOFIYA. Are they sending in troops?

PETRO. Not that. No.

SOFIYA. Christ. Oh Christ.

PETRO. It'll be okay. He'll be okay.

SOFIYA. Tanks as well?

PETRO. They're not sending in the army. No tanks, no soldiers.

SOFIYA. Do you promise?

After a fraction of a moment's thought:

PETRO. Yes. No army. Nothing military.

SOFIYA. Then what?

PETRO. Don't push me, please, not today.

SOFIYA. He just doesn't come first with you, does he?

PETRO. Who?

SOFIYA. Your son – for God's sake. Who else are we talking about?

PETRO. You talk a lot of rubbish these days.

SOFIYA (*continuing*). You've never really cared about him. Never spent time with him. Properly. You don't ever try to understand him.

PETRO. His stupid protests, living in a tent, eating that slop? What's so great to understand?

SOFIYA. He's standing up for the future of this country. Literally. Day by day.

PETRO. The rest of us have to keep the place going. Does he ever think about me? My position?

SOFIYA. Take over a new factory every month, you mean.

PETRO. You're both quite happy to spend the money I bring home. Don't see you refusing it.

SOFIYA. That's cheap. Really cheap.

PETRO (*looking for his jacket*). I have to go and find him.

SOFIYA. You didn't use to be like this.

PETRO. You've changed too, you know that?

SOFIYA. I've listened, that's all.

PETRO. All this – everything that's going on down there – you're so soft.

SOFIYA. All that wonderful money you've earned, do you see what it's done to you?

PETRO. Realistic, that's all, Sofiya. I've just wised up to the times we live in. And I am trying to improve things.

SOFIYA. Sometimes I think you actually preferred the Soviet days.

PETRO. That's almost offensive.

SOFIYA. Your family did okay.

PETRO. We survived. We managed.

SOFIYA. Plenty of people would've been happy to 'survive' like that.

PETRO. Can we just bank this, do you think? For the moment. Until we've got Alex up here. He needs to eat, get washed. That's why we're here, isn't it?

SOFIYA. You have no idea what Alex is doing down there, have you?

PETRO. He's been doing it for weeks, they all have. It hasn't changed anything in months. And it's sure as hell not going to do anything now.

SOFIYA. It has before. It will again.

PETRO. You've spent so long listening to Alex, listening to all his wacko friends, you think we just have to get into Europe and then everything'll be fine. You want us all to stand around in Kiev's central square, sing songs, and that'll make all the problems magically disappear?

SOFIYA. Alex thinks it will.

PETRO. Alex, he has no clue how things work. Alex hasn't got the first idea.

SOFIYA. He's better than either of us. So much braver.

During this PETRO *has redialled, listened. No reply.*

PETRO. I'm going down, into the Maidan. I have to try to find him.

SOFIYA. I'm coming with you.

PETRO. No. Stay. You've got to stay. In case.

And he's speedily out of the door.

SOFIYA (*to the empty room*). In case of what?

Then, again, louder:

In case of what?

She walks over to the window, looks down.

Alex, please, be careful. Please.

Now a sudden knocking on the door.

Petro? Is that you?

But she knows it isn't.

She has to handle this. The knocking continues.

(*At the door.*) Who's there? Who is it?

JAROMIR (*outside the door*). Room service.

SOFIYA. What?

JAROMIR. You ordered room service.

SOFIYA (*now standing at the door*). It's not… I didn't… I didn't get anyone to –

JAROMIR. We have a breakfast tray here for you. Please.

SOFIYA *is opening the door, cautiously.*

But as soon as it's open a crack, JAROMIR *is pushing his way into the room.*

He is followed by another MAN *pushing a trolley, covered largely in a cloth.*

Both men speak with a regional accent.

I'm sorry, we need to come in. Now. Thank you. Thank you.

SOFIYA. What are you doing? Stop! Who are you? What are you – ? You can't just bust your way in here and expect –

The second MAN *firmly shuts the door behind them.* JAROMIR *meanwhile checks the bathroom: it's empty. He turns back to her:*

JAROMIR (*drowning her out*). My name is Jaromir.

He looks at her, asking her to introduce herself. She blanks him.

He indicates the other man (the SNIPER).

I won't – maybe best you don't know his name.

SOFIYA. What are you – who are you?

JAROMIR. Jaromir. And… you?

SOFIYA. I would like you to leave now. Please go. Please just take your trolley and –

The SNIPER *turns on* SOFIYA *threateningly and indicates she should be quiet.*

JAROMIR. It's best – he's right – it's best if you're quiet. He's right.

Terrified, SOFIYA *holds in everything she might say or do. Watching her,* JAROMIR *double-locks the door.*

She watches the SNIPER *go over to the window and throw it open: there is a sudden and major rush of noise from the square below.*

He cautiously pulls back the net curtains and looks out.

Good?

SNIPER. Perfect. Everything they said.

SOFIYA (*trying to pacify them*). My husband, he asked for this side so he could see what's happening. He's a part of – he's an MP actually.

JAROMIR. We know.

SOFIYA. You know.

SNIPER (*looking out*). All the way up to the Cabinet Office, the Parliament. All the way down to the square.

JAROMIR *turns to her:*

JAROMIR. So where is your husband?

SOFIYA. What are you doing here? You can't just –

JAROMIR. Where is your husband? Please tell me now.

SOFIYA (*starting to go*). Right. I'm not tolerating this. I'm going to find someone.

JAROMIR *unholsters/shows a revolver.*

JAROMIR. You need to sit down. Now.

She does not sit.

SOFIYA (*scared but continuing*). Who – who are you?

JAROMIR. Please sit. (*Pointing with the gun.*) Over there.

SOFIYA. I want you to leave.

SNIPER. Sit.

She sits.

JAROMIR *nods at her and goes over to the window.*

(*Looking down.*) Are they going to come up this way?

JAROMIR. Bound to try. What is that, two hundred metres?

SNIPER. One fifty maybe. One eighty.

JAROMIR. That's good.

Then, to their backs:

SOFIYA. He's probably down there.

JAROMIR (*turning back*). Sorry?

SOFIYA. My husband. With my son. Our son. My son is, I mean. My husband is with him. Probably is, I mean.

SNIPER. Your son? He's one of the protesters?

SOFIYA (*realising she shouldn't've mentioned Alex*). I – isn't that why you're here?

JAROMIR. You brought your son here to protest?

SOFIYA (*as if*). Alex joined last year, you know. Plenty of his friends, they've been out since day one, the full three months.

JAROMIR. That's why you're here?

SOFIYA. I could call him. Alright? My husband, I mean, call my husband. (*Beside the bed.*) My phone's just there.

SNIPER. No.

JAROMIR. It's okay. We can wait.

A moment. Then:

SOFIYA. My husband, he's not that important, he's just an –

JAROMIR. Don't make us silence you.

SOFIYA. Are you with Maidan Self-Defence?

SNIPER. Obviously.

At which point, PETRO tries to come in the door only to find it's locked.

He knocks and:

PETRO (*outside*). Sofiya? Sofiya!

SOFIYA. Petro? Petro? You need to –

SNIPER (*silencing her*). Shhh.

She stops immediately.

JAROMIR (*whispering*). Let him in. Go on.

The two men pull to one side, out of sight from the door opening.

PETRO (*continuing, outside*). Sofiya! Are you there? Sofiya!

SOFIYA. Coming. Sorry. I'm coming.

PETRO (*outside*). It's madness down there. Total madness.

She slowly unlocks and opens the door.

There's no point, I couldn't even get through the police cordon – they've got the Berkut guys deployed round the whole hotel.

SOFIYA (*trying to limit what he says*). Come in, shhh, just come in quickly.

PETRO. Why did you lock the door?

SOFIYA. Just come in and then you can tell me everything.

PETRO enters.

He is now carrying two takeaway coffee cups.

PETRO (*continuing*). All I want is for him to come up here today.

Why won't he bloody turn his phone – ?

Now PETRO sees the two men. A short moment.

Then:

Who – Who are you? Sofiya?

JAROMIR. You need to sit down and listen.

PETRO. What the hell are you doing in here? Get out of –

SOFIYA. They've got –

JAROMIR shows the revolver.

JAROMIR. Sit. Please.

PETRO. Sofiya, are you alright? (*Urgent.*) Did they – have they done anything to you?

SOFIYA. No, no, come over here, please, sit down.

PETRO. Have they touched you?

SNIPER. Hey! We're not monsters.

PETRO. You're standing there threatening me and my wife.

JAROMIR. We just want to talk.

PETRO. About what?

JAROMIR. Sit down first, okay? (*Then:*) Okay?

PETRO *slowly sits,* SOFIYA *next to him.*

He is still holding the two coffee cups.

SNIPER (*approaching*). I'll take those. (*The cups.*)

PETRO. That's… I… that's…

SNIPER. Okay, okay, keep one. You share one, we'll share one.

PETRO. Okay. That one… (*The one the* SNIPER *has taken.*) that's black.

SNIPER. That's good. Unless you…

SOFIYA. I'm lactose – you know, milk…

PETRO. She can't… you know.

SNIPER. Okay, swap. Okay?

PETRO. If you're…

SNIPER (*swapping cups*). We just need one. Okay?

PETRO. Okay.

SOFIYA. Okay.

The SNIPER *takes a sip. And then another.*

Meanwhile:

PETRO (*to* SOFIYA). Drink some.

SOFIYA. I can't.

PETRO. Please.

SOFIYA. Stop it. No.

JAROMIR *has meanwhile also taken a sip, watching them. Now:*

JAROMIR. Alright?

PETRO. For what?

SOFIYA. They just forced their way in here, demanding to know where you were.

PETRO. Guys, whoever you are, whoever sent you, I'm just
    one MP, I'm not even in the cabinet, I'm not –

JAROMIR. Everyone knows you're a special one. The
    President gives you deals. He gives you the sweetest deals.

PETRO. I see. Look, I can't get you any special –

SNIPER (*cutting across*). This place, it has to be cleared. It's
    been going since last year. It's dangerous, it's got to finish.
    Today.

PETRO. The President is going to deal with it.

JAROMIR. The whole square. (*Indicating out the window.*)
    The whole Maidan protest camp – the barricades, the tents,
    the pianos, the canteens, the 'libraries', the – all the crazy
    thousands of people will be gone –

PETRO. People – people will get hurt.

JAROMIR (*anger*). Look at it. Crammed with people from Lviv
    and Kherson and Odessa and – That's Kiev's main square,
    the home of government, and it's one huge protest camp,
    shitty people tearing up the cobblestones and throwing them.
    No one knows what they want. They don't even know!

SOFIYA. Actually, it's the new Ukraine. It's a real community
    they've created. Everyone is working together, helping each
    other, building a future.

SNIPER. Your son. With all his crazy people.

PETRO. We came here to try and get him to take a break. In
    fact.

SNIPER. Uh-huh.

SOFIYA. We just want him to –

PETRO (*continuing, over her*). He's been down there over
    a month, maybe a bit longer.

JAROMIR. He comes up here, washes, eats something proper,
    goes back down nice, clean and refreshed, right?

PETRO. Everyone does that. Nearly everyone.

JAROMIR. Doesn't he have a job?

SOFIYA. He's a student. They've given – he's taken time off.

JAROMIR. Kiev National? Taras Shevchenko?

SOFIYA. He's… he's studying at Rotterdam. (*Condescending.*) It's in the Netherlands.

JAROMIR. Got it. (*He too with a smile.*) Europe.

SOFIYA. He won't – he says he can't go back until we have the right country. A normal country.

JAROMIR. That'll happen today. Yanukovych is taking back control. Everything's finally going back to normal.

PETRO. Why are you here? You're not going to get me to – [*talk to anyone important.*]

JAROMIR. Patience, please. We're just waiting for the signal.

SOFIYA. Who are you? You're not from Kyiv, you're not – you don't belong here.

PETRO. What are you doing here? Why do you need to – ?

JAROMIR (*showing his phone*). Waiting. Yes? Now be patient.

PETRO. The square's been cleared before. Last year, again this year. The protesters just come back, more of them, each time.

SNIPER. The police will use bulldozers. Push everything out. And do it properly this time. Fence it off.

PETRO. You can't – you try to push these people, they're going to get hurt, killed. You can just shoot your way in. Send in bulldozers. People will die.

JAROMIR. Only if they refuse to shift.

SOFIYA. Who are you working for? Where are you from?

JAROMIR. We're talking to your husband.

SOFIYA (*snobbery showing through*). Are you from Luhansk, Donetsk? Some where like the East?

JAROMIR. We're trying to have a conversation here – (*With Petro.*)

SOFIYA. Look, this protest, this whole… everyone camped out
in the Maidan down there. It's about making somewhere we
can all –

JAROMIR. Yanukovych was elected President, madam. Your
husband is a member of his party, gets his nice deals from
him.

SOFIYA. My son has been down there since December – he
has rights too. He's – he thought people should actually do
something about it, show they want to create the future we
all deserve.

JAROMIR. It?

SOFIYA. Europe, joining Europe. Making Ukraine a better
place. Proper democracy, a real country, talking to itself.
Ukraine needs to be part of Europe. Is a part of Europe.
I mean, that's how this whole thing started.

JAROMIR. This is a democracy. Right? We have elections?
Yes? We elected Yanukovych as President. So he gets to do
the choosing.

SOFIYA. Yanukovych only got elected because he said
he'd join Europe! Promised. Three months ago, at the
big EU Accession thing – Georgia signs, Moldova signs,
Yanukovych says he won't.

JAROMIR. He had to listen to what Putin was saying. This way
we get to rejoin the Russian Federation.

SOFIYA. The Russians?!

JAROMIR. We can't have independence without Russia.

SOFIYA. We did, in ninety-one. That's twenty-two years ago.
Every region voted *for* independence. Ninety per cent voted
to become independent. Every single oblast wanted it, even
you guys in the East – even Crimea voted for it by sixty per
cent – sixty per cent! It finished the Soviet State!

SNIPER. Only a third of Crimea turned up to vote. And even
then it was only fifty-five per cent.

SOFIYA. Fifty-seven per cent actually.

PETRO (*some surprise*). I never realised you followed all this –
Sofiya?

SOFIYA. What the hell do you know about me these days?
I came here in November, you never knew. Three different
times! You never even asked where I was.

PETRO. What?

SOFIYA. Why do you think Alex came back here?

PETRO. I… you got him to – ?

SOFIYA (*turning back to the* SNIPER, *dogmatic*). Out there,
down in the Maidan, there's all ages, everyone together.
Communists and Nationalists and Muslims and Jews and
everyone. Right now. From every bit of the country. Even
Afghan veterans. Everyone.

SNIPER. All very emotional but President Yanukovych has to
call it a day.

SOFIYA. Of course, you love him. He's one of you.

JAROMIR. You Kiev people, you have no idea what happens in
this country. Never did.

PETRO. What do you mean?

JAROMIR. It's always been like this.

SOFIYA. Always the 'always'!

JAROMIR. Since forever. Back in the Hunger, you left people
like us to die, half my family just –

SOFIYA. Oh please, that – the Holodomor, that was almost
a hundred years ago!

JAROMIR. Feels like yesterday in the Donbas.

SOFIYA. It was the Russians who created the famine! That was
Stalin, his collective farms, so he could export all the grain.
Stalin never cared what happened to Ukrainians.

JAROMIR. Plenty to eat here, in Kiev, though, wasn't there?

SOFIYA. No. There wasn't.

JAROMIR (*continuing, not listening*). You left us to – left my family to die.

PETRO. Look, bad things were done, I know. You're right, plenty of mistakes were made. But we have to put the past behind us. We have to move on and reformulate –

SOFIYA (*exploding at* PETRO). For God's sake, stop that fucking bullshit. Stop humouring them! You're always trying to smooth everything out.

JAROMIR. Wow.

PETRO. I just want to know what they want from me.

JAROMIR. We're waiting. That's all. Any moment, okay? Once they give us the signal.

PETRO. For what? Who are you working for?

JAROMIR. You're in the party, they said you'd understand. That's why we're here.

SOFIYA. Ah, your great Yanukovych. See? He's going to do it all.

JAROMIR. He's not mine. He's the elected President.

SOFIYA. He was Governor of Donetsk – you all gave him a landslide in the East!

SNIPER. Russia has always protected us. We've always been together. Always will do.

SOFIYA. There is no 'always'. Ukraine is growing, changing.

SNIPER. Europe? Those people just want to use Ukraine, get all our stuff and fly off with it. EU's one big runway to tax havens.

JAROMIR. Putin looks after his people. Europe would destroy the Donbas, rip it to shreds. In the Russian Federation, we'll be safe.

SOFIYA. Any Ukraine as long as you get rich?

But she stops as JAROMIR *opens the case he has taken from below the trolley.*

It is a high-powered spotter's scope. PETRO *realises what they're facing:*

PETRO (*seeing this, instantly anxious*). Hey, guys, please, what is this? What exactly are you doing here?

JAROMIR. We need this room. And you'll understand.

PETRO. What are you going to do?

SOFIYA. What is that?

PETRO. You're getting this wrong. Totally wrong. The police aren't going to –

JAROMIR. They said you'd get it. You're in the party, you're bang close to Yanukovych.

PETRO. This was never authorised, this isn't right. Pack up and go. Please.

The SNIPER *steps to the window, looks out.*

JAROMIR. We will receive a call. Then we will do what we came here to do.

PETRO. You've got it wrong. Look – the police, the Berkut Specials I mean, they've only been ordered to fire over their heads. Just to push them back.

SNIPER. It's happening. They've started shooting.

PETRO. They've got yellow armbands, right? The ones with – it's the Berkut who've been issued ammunition.

SNIPER (*looking down*). Yes. Yes.

PETRO. They're only firing warning shots, see?

Meanwhile, SOFIYA *has become totally focused on* PETRO:

SOFIYA. How – how do you know all this?

PETRO does not reply.

JAROMIR has joined the SNIPER *and now sees:*

JAROMIR. No – looks like someone's been hit.

PETRO (*shocked*). What?

SNIPER. Winged. He'll live, I'm guessing.

SOFIYA. Petro? Petro! You knew about this? All this time?

PETRO *shrugs, turns back to her:*

PETRO. That was – that was the phone conference. This morning. Our faction. Well, senior guys in the party. A group call, kind of thing.

SOFIYA. Now the police are out there, shooting everyone? That's what you talked about?

PETRO. It's Berkut. Just them. And they're firing *over* their heads. Pushing them back. That's all we agreed to.

JAROMIR. They're shooting right at the crazies. It's direct line of fire.

SOFIYA. They won't run. You know that. None of them will.

PETRO (*to* JAROMIR). They're ordered to fire over their heads. They said, they told us that was the instruction.

JAROMIR. The police know it's going to take way more than that.

SOFIYA. Alex is down there!

JAROMIR (*seeing*). Another one's gone down.

PETRO. That's not the – (*To* SOFIYA.) Why do you think I wanted to get him up here?

SOFIYA. You didn't, though, did you?

PETRO. He – he's turned his phone off. To stop us.

SOFIYA. Did you message him? Tell him what was about to happen?

PETRO. I couldn't. Couldn't – not that.

SOFIYA. Why not?

PETRO. First, he would've wanted to stay even more. Be with his blessed comrades.

SOFIYA. And second?

A moment. PETRO *looks baffled.*

You said 'first'.

He thinks, then:

PETRO. I couldn't. I can't. I mean, I couldn't. Could I?

SOFIYA. He's our son.

PETRO. I think I know that.

SOFIYA. You've abandoned him.

PETRO. Obviously that's not what I – that's a terrible thing
to say.

SOFIYA. I'm not surprised.

PETRO (*continuing*). To even think it. How can you?

SOFIYA. He gives you a great big factory and you give him
your son. Not a bad deal.

PETRO. I tried to get Alex up here. What else could I do?

SOFIYA. Live the truth, not a lie. How about that?

PETRO. There is no truth. This is politics. This is actual life,
Sofiya.

SOFIYA. The truth is that you'll sell Ukraine to Russia for –
what? A shiny new TV station all of your own? What is it
this time?

PETRO. Everyone in this whole country takes kickbacks.
You've paid them. And taken them. Plenty.

SOFIYA (*continuing*). How much is your son worth to you?
How much are you getting exactly?

PETRO. He's not going to get shot.

SOFIYA. They're out there and the police are armed –

JAROMIR, *at the window looking at the street below,*
announces:

JAROMIR. The police are pulling back. (*Then.*) What the hell
are they doing? They're giving up the street. Handing it right
to them.

SNIPER (*pointing out the window*). They really don't like those petrol bombs. There! Another one. And here come the fireworks. All the usuals.

During this, a couple of small explosions might be heard.

JAROMIR. They're giving up the whole street.

SNIPER. Have we got the go? Come on.

JAROMIR (*as he checks his phone*). Not yet.

PETRO. Can we – can we go? We need to find our son.

JAROMIR. Sit down. Both of you.

SNIPER. We're all in here till the job is done.

SOFIYA (*to* PETRO). You made this happen.

PETRO. Please, don't.

SOFIYA. All these years I've stood by you, tolerated all your – all your deals. The endless compromises.

PETRO. What are you talking about?

SOFIYA. Getting into bed with Yanukovych, taking his bribes.

PETRO. He's getting this country back on its feet. We are. I mean.

At which point, Jaromir's phone rings.

They all fall silent as he answers it:

JAROMIR. Yes?

…Yes. I understand. We're ready.

…Okay.

He hangs up. He looks at the SNIPER.

SNIPER. Yes?

JAROMIR. Standby.

From the lower rack of the trolley, the SNIPER *now pulls a long thin case. He lays it carefully on the bed and opens it: it's a sniper's rifle, which he quickly assembles.*

SOFIYA. Oh my God.

JAROMIR. Really, it's nothing to worry about.

SOFIYA (*terrified, to* PETRO). Are you part of this as well?
Did you agree to this?

PETRO. They didn't tell me anything about. (*Then, quieter.*)
They didn't. Truly.

They can only watch.

The SNIPER *assembles the rifle, adjusting the sights.*

JAROMIR (*to* SNIPER). A couple minutes.

PETRO *looks at* SOFIYA *and decides he has to act.*
He stands, steps towards them:

PETRO. What you're doing, it's wrong.

SNIPER. We're speeding things up. That's all.

PETRO. This is the Kremlin, right? You're taking their orders?
Are they paying you? I'll double it. Any currency, any bank.

SNIPER. You think we're doing this for the money?

PETRO. Triple it. Whatever. Anywhere in the world. Just
name it.

JAROMIR (*not denying it*). Quiet now. Alright? Quiet.

The SNIPER *chambers a bullet and starts to look for*
a target. SOFIYA *watches.*

PETRO. Please. Stop. You can't just shoot people.

JAROMIR. Our orders have been updated.

SOFIYA. Shoot all the protesters, you mean?

PETRO. Sofiya, let me, please, these guys are hard –

JAROMIR (*to* SOFIYA). Quiet.

PETRO. My son is down there. He's not trying to hurt anyone.

JAROMIR. So we'll try not to shoot him.

PETRO (*getting desperate*). Guys, hear me out, the government can handle this. Really can. You start shooting, it's too much, too – it's not what we do.

SOFIYA. You can't just –

PETRO (*harsh*). Sofiya, sit down. (*To* SNIPERS.) Guys, please, Putin's getting this wrong. Please, listen, the President is a realist.

JAROMIR. Maybe. But he's weak. He needs help.

PETRO. I get it. You want everyone shooting at everyone, you want chaos down there, you want blood. That gives Putin an excuse to march in, claim he has to sort it out?

SNIPER. He's too busy in Sochi, he's got his special big Olympics.

PETRO. So why did he send you here?

JAROMIR. We've decided it's time. Alright? Everyone needs to get real.

PETRO. It'll be civil war. Is that what he wants? What you want?

SOFIYA *defiantly walks a couple of paces nearer to them, gets a view out the window.*

SOFIYA. They're not going, are they? The protesters are pushing the police back. They've got, they're using bits of wood as shields.

During this Jaromir's phone pings a message. He checks it:

JAROMIR. We start.

The SNIPER *starts to put the rifle out the window this time.* SOFIYA *reaches to pull the rifle back.*

SNIPER. No, no!

JAROMIR. Stop, you mustn't do that.

They are now in a tussle.

JAROMIR *turns to* PETRO:

Come on, stop her. Petro!

SOFIYA (*turning back to* PETRO). For God's sake, do something!

Help me stop them!

PETRO. What? What can we do? These people are crazy.

JAROMIR *pulls her back.*

JAROMIR. Just sit down. Yes?

PETRO. Sofiya, please. Come sit down.

The SNIPER *is now aiming and he fires.*

It's a precise, 'technical' noise, not hugely loud. He immediately pulls the rifle in.

The room falls silent.

JAROMIR *is looking down at the street through his scope.*

JAROMIR. He's wounded. He's moving.

The SNIPER *chambers a bullet and starts to take aim again but* SOFIYA *strides over and tries to grab the rifle again.*

SOFIYA. This has to stop now. You have to stop!

JAROMIR. Petro, come on!

PETRO *doesn't move.*

The SNIPER *and* SOFIYA *go on tussling over the rifle.*

For God's sake!

This time the SNIPER *slaps* SOFIYA *hard across the face. She falls back onto the floor.*

PETRO *stands but doesn't move forwards. A silence in the room.*

The SNIPER *looks at* SOFIYA.

And then goes over and picks up her mobile phone from beside the bed.

SNIPER. Here.

SOFIYA *remains looking down.*

Sofiya! Here. Your phone.

She looks up.

Call your son. Alright? This is for you. Call him, get him to take cover, get out of there. Then you let us carry on. Okay? Here.

SOFIYA *starts to reach up for the phone.*

She is intending to take it but then slows down. She cannot. Something is stopping her.

She drops her hand and then very quietly:

SOFIYA. I... I can't.

PETRO. Sofiya?

SOFIYA (*gaining volume*). No. I can't. No.

JAROMIR. Call him. Right now. He can get himself somewhere safe. He'll be okay.

SOFIYA (*sickened by what she has to do*). I... I can't do that.

PETRO. Call him, Sofiya, he might answer this time. If it's you ringing him.

SOFIYA. It's – yes, he might. He really might. But... (*Pained.*) I'm sorry.

I'm so so sorry.

SNIPER. Take the phone. Call him!

SOFIYA (*continuing*). I mean I can't. I mean, I suppose I mean I shouldn't. (*She looks at* PETRO.) We mustn't. Right?

PETRO. Sofiya? What the hell are you doing?

SOFIYA. He needs to do this. They all do, all of them down there. So we have to let him. This is his fight. He came back here because he knew he had to. Don't you see – you must?

JAROMIR. What?

SOFIYA. This is – (*Tearfully pushing the phone away.*) please, stop that – this is – my son is fighting for the new Ukraine. He – and all the others down there – he *is* Ukraine. They all are. This is a battle that has to be fought. By him. Whatever the price.

A moment, then:

PETRO. She's right. (*Then:*) She is right.

SNIPER. Call him!

SOFIYA (*more settled*). I wouldn't do that to him. I can't. I won't.

SNIPER. I am telling you to call your son.

SOFIYA. And you, both of you, you're helping him make Ukraine.

SNIPER. You're crazy. You are just crazy.

As he turns to find another target

SOFIYA (*now finding defiance*). Every shot you fire, it's just going to make it happen sooner.

JAROMIR. It's going to be a very bad day down there.

PETRO. It's – it's what they've been waiting for.

And the lights slowly dim.

End.

FIVE DAY WAR

David Edgar

Characters

ECHO
POLINA
YULIA, *her daughter*
FOXTROT
INDIA
VICTOR

Setting

The play is set in a hunting lodge in a forest, north-west of Kyiv, Ukraine, between 23 and 28 February 2022.

Scene One

*Wednesday 23 February. A room in what will turn out to be
a hunting lodge in a forested area of north-central Ukraine.
On a side table, there is one old-fashioned landline telephone.
On the wall, a box of ten room keys, most of which have gone.
A middle-aged woman,* POLINA, *and her twelve-year-old
daughter* YULIA *are looking at a man standing with two
large suitcases and a shoulder bag. He carries a blindfold.
The man is code-named* ECHO. POLINA *has a clipboard with
photographs of guests she's expecting.*

ECHO. YA pershyy?

POLINA. Beg pardon?

ECHO. YA pershyy?

POLINA. Beg pardon?

ECHO. Am I the first?

POLINA. Hardly.

She looks at her list.

Now, you are…?

ECHO. Uh, I can't remember.

POLINA (*looking*). Um…

ECHO. I mean, I'm actually…

POLINA. Shh. Ah, yes.

She ticks a picture.

Room Six. Second floor.

YULIA *takes the key from the box, as* ECHO *looks bleakly
at his heavy luggage.*

I'm Polina, this is Yulia. Breakfast is at oh-eight-hundred hours, sheets and towels are changed every three days. No firearms in the rooms.

YULIA (*giving the key to* ECHO). Anti-clockwise.

ECHO. Right.

He pockets the blindfold. Enter FOXTROT.

POLINA. Tea? Coffee? Vodka?

ECHO. Tea.

FOXTROT. Vodka.

POLINA *looks at* ECHO.

ECHO. Vodka. Dyakuyu.

POLINA. And we like to speak in Russian.

ECHO. Oh, right. Sorry.

(*Now speaking Russian.*) Vodka, thank you.

FOXTROT *a private smile.* POLINA *and* YULIA *turn out front.*

POLINA. Wednesday.

YULIA. The day before it all began.

POLINA. During which our dear guests arrive,

YULIA. Assess their situation,

POLINA. And wonder what they're doing here.

POLINA *and* YULIA *go out.*

FOXTROT (*re:* ECHO*'s large suitcases*). You've come prepared.

ECHO. Um, I didn't know…

FOXTROT. They told me, five days max.

ECHO. So at least, clean sheets.

FOXTROT *a quizzical look.*

FOXTROT. No phones.

ECHO. Except for that one.

FOXTROT *picks up the phone, tries to get a dialling tone. Nothing.*

FOXTROT. So what have you been told?

ECHO. What have you been told?

FOXTROT. I've been told what you've been told. For now.

They enjoy the moment.

ECHO. In fact, I think we've met.

FOXTROT. So you are...?

ECHO. I'm Acting Interim Deputy Director of the Rural Housing Division of the Regional Council of Dnipropetrovsk.

FOXTROT. Only Interim?

ECHO. But Acting.

FOXTROT. It's possible we've met. I was spokesman for Construction for a while. In the national parliament, of course.

ECHO. So do we know, who else...?

FOXTROT. Largely Opposition Bloc people. The usual suspects.

ECHO. Not usual to me.

FOXTROT. Yes, I did wonder what an Acting Deputy is doing / in a –

ECHO. You tell me.

FOXTROT. And what the fuck is going on.

Enter INDIA, *with a sensible suitcase.*

INDIA. Oh, you.

FOXTROT. Well, if it isn't Val/entina –

INDIA. No it isn't.

She puts her hand out to ECHO, *as* YULIA *enters with a tray of vodkas and biscuits for the men.*

It's India. And you are?

YULIA *puts down the tray and gets* INDIA *her key.*

FOXTROT. He's Acting Interim –

ECHO. I'm Echo.

FOXTROT. 'Echo'.

ECHO. Yes, it's the –

FOXTROT (*'*ECHO*' tone*). Ecc-oh…

ECHO. Oh, I see. Yes.

INDIA (*to* FOXTROT). And you are?

FOXTROT (*with a shrug*). Foxtrot.

YULIA. Tea? Coffee?

FOXTROT. And there's vodka.

INDIA. Well, surprise surprise. Tea, please.

YULIA (*handing* INDIA *her key*). The names are from the NATO alphabet. Alpha, Bravo, Charlie, et cetera. Room three, first floor. I'm Yulia.

INDIA. Thank you.

YULIA *goes out.*

Presumably, it's 'know your enemy'.

ECHO. Or spell him, anyway.

VICTOR *enters. He's the youngest of the men.*

VICTOR. Ah, here you are.

Looking questioningly at ECHO*'s bags.*

Um…

ECHO. Somebody told me…

VICTOR. Everyone's here now. From 'Alpha' to 'Yankee'. I'm sure you're all eager for a briefing.

INDIA. Yes.

VICTOR. Which I'll be giving after dinner.

FOXTROT. And you are? Tango? Whiskey?

VICTOR. Victor.

FOXTROT. Ah. The FSB?

VICTOR *a quizzical smile.* FOXTROT *sits, firmly.*

Then I think we'd like to know what's going on, right now.

INDIA *and* ECHO *don't sit but they don't go out either.*

VICTOR. You mean, what you're all here for?

ECHO. Uh…

INDIA. Well, I'd assumed…

FOXTROT. Come on. We all know why we're *here*. With the silly names and blindfolds and giving up our phones. We're here to be the inner cabinet of the next government of Ukraine.

Pause.

Correct?

VICTOR. Yes.

FOXTROT. So what we need to know, is why and when and how.

VICTOR *gestures to* INDIA *and* ECHO *to sit, which they do.*

VICTOR. Two days ago President Putin chaired a meeting of the Russian Security Council to consider requests from the people's republics of the Donbas – Donetsk and Luhansk – for the recognition of their independence. And, in view of the current genocide being waged against them by the illegitimate, criminal and neo-Nazi Kiev junta, to come to their defence. If necessary.

FOXTROT. So that means…

VICTOR. Obviously, it would be impossible to stop the genocide without overthrowing the body perpetrating it.

INDIA. So, when…?

VICTOR. I will give a detailed briefing every morning.

FOXTROT. So *you've* got a / phone –

ECHO. I skil'ky chasu tse vse tryvatyme?

ECHO *has slipped into Ukrainian. They all look at him.*

(*Apologetically, back in Russian.*) How long will this all take?

VICTOR. You are in a hunting lodge in what you can see is a dense forest area approximately forty-eight kilometres north west of Kiev. We expect the junta to fall within five days. Hence asking you to come prepared for all sartorial eventualities. I hope you've all brought decent suits. And where appropriate, parade uniforms.

ECHO. What for?

VICTOR. Parades.

ECHO *is suddenly pleased about his luggage. A gong sounds.*

Now dinner. Meeting everybody else. You'll know most of them.

ECHO, FOXTROT *and* INDIA *stand.*

FOXTROT. And what's that phone for?

ECHO. It doesn't work.

VICTOR. It only has to, once.

INDIA. To summon us to Kiev.

VICTOR. Precisely.

INDIA, ECHO *and* FOXTROT *go out.* YULIA *enters with tea for* INDIA.

YULIA. Uh-oh.

VICTOR. They've gone to dinner. So is it just you and your mother?

YULIA. Her name's Polina. Dad's on a trip. My sister's staying with a schoolfriend in a little town near Kiev.

VICTOR. Has your sister ever ridden on a tank?

YULIA. Don't think so. Why?

Enter FOXTROT.

VICTOR. Foxtrot.

FOXTROT. So that's who we are, and why. What are we actually supposed to do here, for five days?

VICTOR. Prepare for government.

YULIA. Wow.

Scene Two

Thursday 24 February.

YULIA *(out front)*. Thursday. Day One.

POLINA. The discovery that Yankee has an allergy to fish.

YULIA. First briefing.

POLINA. What Is Going On?

> *The gong sounds.* VICTOR *is giving his morning briefing. He has notes. Sitting and watching are* INDIA, FOXTROT *and* ECHO; *we imagine other Ministers-in-Waiting also sitting by.* POLINA *and* YULIA *standing.* ECHO's *luggage has gone, a map of Ukraine is on an easel, with arrows indicating Russian advances on seven fronts. Some detritis – bottles, glasses, plates – from the previous evening.*

VICTOR. At oh-four-hundred hours this morning a force of nearly two hundred thousand troops in nine battalion battle groups crossed the Russian, Belarusian and Crimean borders into Ukraine. To our north, a pincer movement is moving south along two axes to encircle Kiev. This force includes advanced air assault groups born by helicopter, who are now securing the Airport at Hostomel, lightly defended by around two hundred low-echelon conscript Ukrainians. Once captured, the airport will receive airborne troops in ever greater numbers and serve as a hub for operations against Kiev, to its south-east. At oh-six-hundred hours President Putin broadcast this statement.

He plays a section of PUTIN*'s speech on his phone. We hear it rendered in English.*

PUTIN. ' – a decision to carry out a special military operation. The purpose of this operation is to protect people who, for eight years now, have been facing humiliation and genocide perpetrated by the Kiev regime. To this end, we will seek to demilitarise and denazify Ukraine. It is not our plan to – '

VICTOR *stops the playback.*

VICTOR. So, in summary, the army of the Russian Federation / is advancing –

FOXTROT. What's not the plan?

VICTOR. I'm sorry?

FOXTROT. The President was saying 'It is not the plan to'. What's not the plan?

After a moment, VICTOR *restarts the tape:*

PUTIN. ' – to occupy Ukrainian territory. We do not intend to impose anything on anyone by force.'

VICTOR *stops the playback.* POLINA *and* YULIA *step forward.*

VICTOR. So that's all clear.

Scene Three

Friday 25 February. Morning. The gong.

POLINA. Friday. Day Two.

YULIA. We're out of gherkins.

POLINA. Sierra wants his parade uniform pressing.

YULIA. Second Briefing.

POLINA. In which India asks another tricky question.

   VICTOR*'s Friday briefing to the same group.*

VICTOR. In the Donbas region in the east and in the southern
   regions north of Crimea, Russian forces continue to advance
   speedily. Special forces are undertaking operations directed
   against the junta in Kiev. It remains our expectation that
   Ukrainian forces will lay down their arms and our brave
   boys will be met by cheering crowds strewing flowers in
   their path.

INDIA. May I ask a question?

VICTOR. Yes, of course.

INDIA. Did you take the Airport from the conscripts?
   Are troops landing there? Like you said would happen,
   yesterday?

VICTOR. We recaptured the airfield after a short battle. I should
   point out that the Russian airforce outnumbers the Ukrainian
   by thirty to one.

Scene Four

Friday 25 February. Afternoon.

YULIA. While later on that day:

POLINA. Foxtrot reports to India on a Helpful Little Chat he
had with Victor.

YULIA. And India has hers.

POLINA. Her?

YULIA. Little chat.

>	FOXTROT *stands looking at the map.* INDIA *enters,
>	looking at the bottles and glasses with distaste.* FOXTROT
>	waves the bottle.*

FOXTROT. Drink?

INDIA. No thank you.

FOXTROT. Toasting our success.

INDIA. I thought that was last night.

FOXTROT. Our further success.

INDIA (*dryly*). Yes.

>	*She sits.*

FOXTROT. So what are you doing? Apart from waiting?

INDIA. We were told to master our briefs.

FOXTROT. Have you got a brief?

INDIA. Not yet.

>	*She sits down.*

FOXTROT. Got your eye on anything?

INDIA. I am keen to serve my country.

FOXTROT. Yeah, sure, me too.

INDIA. Oh?

>	*Slight pause.*

>	Fair enough.

FOXTROT *sits.*

FOXTROT. So we know that Sergei – 'Alpha' – has been offered Agriculture and the Environment, suitable as his businesses exploit the first and threaten the second. 'Sierra''s got his eye on Defence, probably because he spends his weekends, as you may know, dressing up in military uniform and re-enacting battles from the Napoleonic wars. And Yankee's obviously in line for Internal, as everybody knows he's been a full-time FSB asset since Putin came to power in 1999.

INDIA. Cynical. And you?

FOXTROT. Well, in my little chat with 'Victor' I said I might be right for Sport and Culture. Or even Finance.

INDIA. Depending I guess whether your primary interest is your football team or your bank. Since Zelensky closed it down.

FOXTROT (*spreading his hands*). And me the cynic. We're all from the productive sections of the country. Even Echo.

INDIA. Yes, Echo. He's from where?

FOXTROT. Dnipropetrovsk. But I presume his family's from the countryside.

INDIA. How do you know that?

FOXTROT. You heard. He says 'dyakuyu' for 'thank you'.

INDIA. Yes. But you didn't raise the big ones.

FOXTROT. Big ones?

INDIA. The big jobs. In your 'little chat with Victor'…

Pause.

Of course, it was a confidential conversation.

ECHO *comes in.*

Good morning.

ECHO. Morning.

ECHO *goes to the map. He runs his finger up from Crimea northwards. Then he breathes a little.*

FOXTROT. What're you looking for?

ECHO. Oh, I… nothing.

He goes out.

FOXTROT. So how d'you really think it's going?

INDIA. What's going?

FOXTROT (*obvious*). The invasion.

INDIA. 'Special military – '

BOTH. 'Operation'.

FOXTROT. Did you spot, 'Victor' said they'd *re*-captured the airfield. And he didn't say anything about landing troops.

INDIA. What do you mean?

FOXTROT. Well, what happened between capture and re-capture?

INDIA. Thirty-to-one superiority. Cheering crowds. And don't you think it's a little early for defeatism?

FOXTROT *stands.*

FOXTROT. I'm not defeatist. I just like to know what's going on. (*He makes to go.*)

INDIA. So what happened, in your conversation?

FOXTROT. Confidential, as you say.

INDIA. Well, sure. As you say.

Slight pause. FOXTROT *sits down again.*

FOXTROT. Well, he asked me what I wanted.

INDIA. And you said?

FOXTROT. Well, I asked him if the top jobs were still open.

INDIA. Not too pushy?

FOXTROT. Well, he said the matter wasn't finalised.

INDIA. And then?

FOXTROT. He smiled.

INDIA. 'Smiled'. And?

FOXTROT. And changed the subject.

INDIA. Oh, what to?

FOXTROT. He asked, what I thought was the main point of the operation, And I said, the threat of NATO at our borders. The frontier between America and Russia is Ukraine.

INDIA. And he liked that?

FOXTROT. Well, that's the interesting thing. He moved on to something else.

INDIA. Again.

FOXTROT. And asked about the people they'd approached, like us, but who'd refused to join. And what ought to be done with them.

INDIA. What did you say?

FOXTROT. I said, arrest them. Jail them. Chuck away the key. Cos after all, whatever Putin says, we are at war. But I'm not sure that was what he wanted. So I said, what would *he* do? And he laughed and said he liked us to ask tricky questions.

INDIA. Oh.

FOXTROT. As you did, in the meeting, obviously. Silver star.

INDIA. And then –

Enter VICTOR.

VICTOR. Ah, Foxtrot.

FOXTROT. Victor.

VICTOR (*with a gesture towards* INDIA). Might you…?

FOXTROT. Sure.

He stands.

Good luck.

He's gone.

INDIA. So is this our little chat?

VICTOR *smiles and sits, opening a notebook.*

VICTOR. Three things.

He'll take notes.

As you know, there's thinking about jobs.

INDIA. Yes.

VICTOR. So we're asking people what they'd like to do.

INDIA. Well, obviously, to serve my country.

VICTOR. Obviously.

INDIA. In national government, I had senior roles. Finance.

VICTOR. Junior Minister. And before that, Kharkov, Culture.
    Most successfully.

INDIA. Well, yes.

VICTOR. It's a great idea.

INDIA *decides to take the plunge.*

INDIA. But the top jobs are still open?

VICTOR. Why do you ask?

Clearly INDIA *has asked the wrong thing.*

INDIA. It doesn't matter. Second question?

VICTOR. You'll know we approached people like yourself,
    who we hoped would wish to serve their country.

INDIA. Yes, of course.

VICTOR. Not everyone agreed to do that.

INDIA. No.

VICTOR. And I wondered what you felt should be done. With
    such people. Afterwards.

INDIA. Well, I'd imagine the new government would want to
    seem magnanimous.

VICTOR. Oh, really? Do you think so?

He writes something down.

INDIA. But it's a tricky question.

VICTOR. Yes.

INDIA. But you might like tricky questions.

VICTOR. Not in front of everyone. The dangers of defeatism.

INDIA (*wrong again*). Right.

VICTOR *stands.*

VICTOR. Well, thank you.

INDIA. And the third? Third question?

VICTOR. Oh, I think we've covered all the / ground –

INDIA (*deciding to go for it*). Look, we can all count. There's
four jobs you haven't filled. Including the top two.

VICTOR. Yes?

INDIA. I would like to be considered, not just for Culture. If
that doesn't seem too – pushy.

Pause.

VICTOR. Obviously, the top job isn't – just about the brief.

INDIA. No, of course not. The new – top person would need to
justify our taking over to the world.

VICTOR. And, if –

INDIA. And of course, yes, it's about NATO moving east. In
blatant violation of its promises. But for me the key thing is
what happened in 2014.

VICTOR. Which was?

INDIA. An armed coup by fascists in our capital, and those
fascists heading straight off to commit genocide against my
Russian-speaking kith and kin in the Donbas.

Slight pause.

VICTOR (*standing*). Of course, yes.

INDIA. And?

VICTOR. We'll see.

Scene Five

Saturday 26 February. VICTOR *moves away. Enter* POLINA *and* YULIA.

POLINA (*out front*). Saturday.

YULIA. Sheet-changing day.

POLINA. Always revealing.

YULIA. Day Three.

> *The gong.* VICTOR *is addressing the wider group, from notes. We see* INDIA, FOXTROT, *and* ECHO *sitting, watching.* POLINA *and* YULIA *also stand watching.*

VICTOR. To the north east of the capital, the forces of the Russian Federation have passed Chernihiv on their way to Kiev. To the north west of Kiev, a mighty convoy now approaches the suburbs of Bucha and Irpin and the gateway to the capital itself.

> *Pause.*

And if there are no questions –

ECHO. What's happening in Kharkiv?

FOXTROT. Kharkov.

ECHO. Kharkov.

VICTOR. Fierce fighting is continuing in Ukraine's second city. It is expected –

ECHO. Has the junta fallen in Kiev?

VICTOR. It remains an expectation that this is imminent.

ECHO. Is the plan of special military operation, not an invasion not occupying territory, to invade and occupy Dnipropetrovsk?

VICTOR. I think that depends… on what you mean by 'occupy'.

As the scene breaks, INDIA *speaks bitterly to* FOXTROT.

INDIA. Smiles if you're pushy. Be nice to people who refused to join us. Just loves tricky questions.

FOXTROT. What?

INDIA (*sarcastic*). Thanks for the helpful advice.

FOXTROT *smiles and shrugs.* INDIA *exits angrily, followed by* FOXTROT, YULIA *and* POLINA, *leaving* ECHO *and* VICTOR.

VICTOR. Good question.

ECHO. What?

VICTOR. Dnipropetrovsk. Why d'you ask it?

ECHO. I'm sorry, look. It doesn't matter.

VICTOR. Come come.

ECHO. It's just… In Putin's meeting with the council one of them implied the plan was to make the 'independent republics' part of Russia. Putin shut him up.

VICTOR. That's not the plan at present.

ECHO. So what's the future? Kharkov, Odessa back with the Motherland? Dnipropetrovsk, part of, what do they say, a vassal state?

VICTOR. That's not the plan at present.

ECHO. What did Putin say? The break up of the Soviet Union, the greatest disaster of the century?

VICTOR. 'Catastrophe'.

ECHO. Catherine the Great said Ukraine was 'Little Russia'.

VICTOR. The President does not think he's Catherine the Great.

ECHO. Oh no?

Pause.

It's just, if I'm to be part of this, I need to know what 'this' this is.

VICTOR. Of course you're part of this.

ECHO. There's people asking why I'm here at all. Why me.

VICTOR. You're here because you are essential to the operation. How 'this' will be presented to the world. The dramaturgy.

ECHO. The dramawhat?

VICTOR. In America, the governor of a minor state has a massively ambitious wife who forces him to run for President. Then he deceives her with a White House intern and she turns from Lady Macbeth into a victim of male chauvinism and a women's liberation icon.

ECHO. Um... how does / that – ?

VICTOR. In Britain, an intelligent and sensitive young prince is married off to a pretty airhead. But within a decade she transforms herself into a feminist campaigner who hugs AIDS victims and fights landmines and has been betrayed by an egghead geek adulterer who hugs trees.

ECHO. Where is this / going?

VICTOR. While in this country, just eight years ago, a pro-Russian President resiles on his commitment to join Europe and is overthrown by heroic patriots in the capital's main square. Or – what actually happened – a democratically elected leader's ousted by a violent insurrection led by fascist nationalists who then lead battalions of mercenaries eastward to suppress the people of the Donbas who want the President who they elected back.

ECHO. I still don't quite / follow what –

VICTOR. But most importantly of all. Eighty years ago. A country is invaded from the west. The invaders are supported by local Nazis who kill patriots who are trying to resist this brutal occupation. The invaders set up a puppet administration under foreign control. But eventually the armies of the east come to the rescue, not to occupy but to liberate the country. So what does that remind you of?

ECHO. Yes, well, there may be parallels / between –

VICTOR. Tell me about Pavel Sergeyevich.

ECHO. My grandfather?

VICTOR. Of course.

ECHO. Well, he fought in the Great Patriotic War.

VICTOR. He died in the Great Patriotic War. Retaking Dnipropetrovsk, the capital of your region, from the German occupiers. Having lost his Jewish wife and child to the Ukrainian Nationalist collaborators. And I'd imagine their last words – how wondrous it would be to hear them – were in their native tongue. Your native tongue. Ukrainian.

Slight pause.

You're right. There is one difference, from then to now. Yes, the Red Army liberated occupied Ukraine from brutal tyranny, but no one can say what followed was true freedom. But this time, we Russians don't just bring you bread and salt. But the gifts of human rights, constitutional government, and democracy. A Ukraine in which all cultures and all tongues can co-exist in freedom.

ECHO. Well…

VICTOR. That's the dramaturgy. That's the story. Your narrative, your language. That's why you.

Scene Six

Sunday 27 February. YULIA *and* POLINA *enter with evidence of a good night of drinking and eating. Dotting it about the room.*

YULIA. Sunday.

POLINA. Second Floor Toilet Blocked.

YULIA. Five glasses and a decanter smashed.

POLINA. All in all, I'd prefer the wild-boar people.

YULIA. Day Four.

> VICTOR, ECHO, FOXTROT *and* INDIA. INDIA *looks at the bottles with a little distaste.* YULIA *and* POLINA *go.*

FOXTROT. It's just the three of us?

> VICTOR *closes the door and gestures for the* THREE *to sit, which they do.*

VICTOR. And I wonder what you have in common?

FOXTROT. We don't know what we're doing.

VICTOR. Yet you've worked out what jobs are available. And you don't really have your eye on Sport and Culture.

ECHO. So what's going to happen?

> VICTOR *sits.*

VICTOR (*to* ECHO). How would you describe the events of early 2014 in Central Kiev?

ECHO. A violent insurrection.

VICTOR. Followed by?

INDIA. A coup d'état.

VICTOR. And the status of the regime which took over?

FOXTROT. Illegitimate.

VICTOR. So, constitutionally, who is currently the President of Ukraine?

ECHO. The last person to be legitimately elected to that office?

FOXTROT. What?

INDIA. Yanukovych?

VICTOR *has a piece of paper.*

FOXTROT. You can't mean, Yanukovych coming back.

VICTOR (*reads*). 'Fellow Ukrainians. I am Viktor Fedorovych
Yanukovych, the last person to be constitutionally elected
President of our country, speaking to you from Kiev.'

ECHO *looks surprised,* INDIA *and* FOXTROT *look
disbelieving.*

In a manner of speaking.

VICTOR *reads on.*

'I must inform you that a judge of the Supreme Court
has ruled that the current government is unconstitutional,
illegitimate, and illegal.'

INDIA. The judge?

VICTOR. The last Yanukovych-appointed judge still in office.
(*He reads on.*)

'I have to tell you, that government has now fled.'

The three look surprised.

Or – 'that government has been detained'. Or – 'The present
whereabouts of that government is unknown.'

FOXTROT. Hm.

VICTOR. 'Accordingly, and pending new elections, I am
dissolving the current parliament…'

FOXTROT. No doubt at gunpoint.

VICTOR. '…and am appointing an emergency new
government. Due to my age and sadly my infirmity – '

INDIA *makes the drinking gesture.*

' – that government will be headed by an Acting Interim
President, to ensure that constitutional order is restored,
I have invited forces of the Russian Federation to assist in
preserving order.'

Pause to let it sink in.

'Please stay in your houses and follow the instructions of the authorities. Glory to Ukraine.'

Pause.

INDIA. And we have to justify that?

VICTOR *stands*.

VICTOR. One of you. Which we will practise here tomorrow. You have this evening to prepare.

He makes to go.

FOXTROT (*standing*). So speaking of the government, how's the fleeing actually going?

VICTOR. We must prepare for all eventualities.

He goes out.

INDIA (*to* FOXTROT, *gesturing at the bottles*). You might consider switching to the tea. If you're serious about running the country.

ECHO. So what's tomorrow? A rehearsal?

FOXTROT. 'One of us'. It's an audition.

Scene Seven

Monday 28 February. POLINA *and* YULIA *enter to clear up and put out chairs and a table for the simulation of a press conference. A water glass on the table.* ECHO *is there.* YULIA *listens to the conversation as she tidies.*

POLINA. Monday.

YULIA. Day Five.

POLINA. We hear something of Polina.

She turns to ECHO.

Good morning, Mr Echo.

ECHO. Oh, Mikhail, please. Can I give you a hand?

POLINA. Thanks very much.

ECHO *starts to help.*

ECHO. Is it just you who runs the lodge?

POLINA. My husband's gone abroad, to Serbia.

ECHO. Oh, why?

POLINA. He was frightened that he'd be called up.

ECHO. I guess he would be.

POLINA. But then, it'll all be over in three weeks.

ECHO. They said, five days.

POLINA. The boss says there's a sixty-kilometre convoy stretching from the Belarus border to the outskirts of the city.

ECHO. And is that a good thing?

POLINA. People strewing flowers. Girls riding on tanks.

ECHO. To welcome our heroic allies, bringing freedom and democracy.

POLINA. To this nonsense country. I'm not sure we deserve it.

ECHO. Nonsense?

POLINA. What do you call a country where there's a change of party at every presidential election?

ECHO. Well, I guess…

POLINA. And at the last one we get a little Jewish comic. Who says the Nazis killed his great grandparents and his grandfather fought with the Red Army.

ECHO. Yes?

POLINA. So why's he so angry at the Russian army now?

ECHO. Well, they say he's going to flee. If he hasn't fled already.

POLINA. Oh, come on. You think our boys will let him get away?

ECHO. You mean…

POLINA *gives the throat-slit gesture.* VICTOR *enters, followed by* INDIA *and* FOXTROT.

VICTOR. Ah, thank you. Shall we make a start?

Scene Eight

POLINA. Later that morning.

YULIA. Foxtrot, Echo and India rehearse.

POLINA. And we learn more of everyone.

POLINA *moves to her place, as –*

YULIA. Including Yulia.

The rehearsal of a press conference. FOXTROT *is sat at the table, coming to the end of his turn. He has notes and is well-prepared.* VICTOR, INDIA *and* ECHO *sit watching.*

FOXTROT. You listen to the people who would ban the Russian language from our schools and offices. People who insult that language as the speech of rock and roll and criminals. Who don't think people should be allowed to marry in the language they proposed in. In fact, the language of the people of the Rus – this Rus – for a thousand years.

The WATCHERS *applaud.*

Next question.

VICTOR. What is your opinion of western sanctions? Are you worried by this threat?

FOXTROT. Our heroic allies have managed without Italian ham and French cheese ever since the liberation of Crimea. I'm sure we can manage without American Fried Chicken.

INDIA. Kentucky.

FOXTROT. Without Kentucky Chicken now.

VICTOR *turns to* ECHO, *who doesn't have a question.* INDIA *jumps in.*

INDIA. Mr 'Acting President'. You call the Russian invasion a 'special operation'. You have surrounded and – I presume – taken the capital. How is this not an invasion?

FOXTROT. Well, uh, because…

VICTOR. Limited objective.

FOXTROT. The operation has the limited objective of denazifying and demilitising – militarising / the –

INDIA. Yet the governments of the West have universally condemned Russia's actions as invading a sovereign foreign country. What is your reaction to this charge?

VICTOR *finds a pre-written note and takes it to* FOXTROT.

FOXTROT (*fumbling with his notes*). My reaction is… that, for all their bluster, is it not noteworthy… ah…uh…

VICTOR *lays the note in front of* FOXTROT.

(*Reading the note.*) Ah. I have a piece of news for you. The former government including the self-styled President Zelensky have fled to Lvov, heartland of neo-Nazi nationalism. They will feel comfortable there.

POLINA *claps enthusiastically. The others follow.* FOXTROT *knocks back the water.*

VICTOR (*to* ECHO). Now Mr Acting President the Second.

FOXTROT *and* ECHO *change places.*

ECHO. Is there more water?

YULIA *replenishes the water from a jug.*

VICTOR. Can you explain what the Russian Federation means by 'denazification'?

ECHO. It means removing neo-Nazis from all institutions, including the civil service, local government and of course the army. Oh, sorry, first, removing the government that is the successor of the one imposed in a neo-Nazi coup. Which has happened now.

Slight pause.

With our government of freedom, democracy and human rights. Next?

FOXTROT. Acting President. Do you consider Crimea part of Russia?

ECHO. Yes.

FOXTROT. So an attack on Crimea would be an attack on Russia.

ECHO. Uh… yes.

FOXTROT. And if the Donbas people decided to join Russia? That would be part of Russia too?

ECHO. Yes, I suppose so. But…

FOXTROT. And if NATO troops attacked them?

ECHO. That's a – what do they say, kind of question?

VICTOR *is finding the note he will give to* ECHO.

VICTOR. Hypothetical.

FOXTROT. Meaning, 'I don't have to answer'?

VICTOR *prepares to give* ECHO *a note and* INDIA *takes over questioning:*

INDIA. So can I ask how long you expect to be this so-called Acting President?

ECHO. Not very long.

INDIA. How long's 'not very long'?

ECHO. As long as it might take to / make the necessary –

INDIA. So is it really a temporary government devoted to democracy and human rights? Or is it an unelected, junta who have seized power through force and will use force to keep it?

ECHO. What, you're saying it's not / really –

INDIA. I'm not saying anything. It's just a question. Unless you think it's 'hypothetical'.

ECHO *reaches for the water and knocks it over.*

ECHO. Shit.

VICTOR *decides not to give* ECHO *the note but* INDIA *snatches it, and takes it to* ECHO. *Simultaneously,* POLINA *and* YULIA *are clearing the water and pouring another glass.*

Beg pardon, I…

INDIA (*giving* ECHO *the note*). Go on.

ECHO *looks to* VICTOR, *who has no choice but to gesture him to read it.*

ECHO. I have… I have been told… that the self-styled President, the former President… um, crossfire…

(*To* INDIA.) You're so good at questions. Try answering.

YULIA *goes out to fill up the water jug.* INDIA *goes to the table, sits and reads the note.*

INDIA. 'I have sober news. This morning a unit of the Russian special forces located the self-styled President and his entourage and attempted peacefully to detain him. Unfortunately his security detail responded with deadly force and Zelensky and his team and family were caught in crossfire. While this incident is a matter of regret' – great regret – 'responsibility lies entirely with the illegal Ukrainian government.' Next?

FOXTROT. So has this actually / happened?

VICTOR *shakes his head, obviously not, as* ECHO *interrupts.*

ECHO. So what is this? A botched arrest? Or an assassination?

INDIA. It's neither. It's what happens in a war.

ECHO. So suddenly this is a war?

INDIA. I mean, a military / operation.

ECHO. You claim since independence Ukraine is not a functioning democracy. Yet every election bar one has seen a change of government.

INDIA. Oh, is that evidence of / functioning –

FOXTROT (*to rescue*). On the other / hand –

ECHO. How unlike Russia.

INDIA. It's evidence of instability and corruption.

FOXTROT. May I ask –

ECHO. Putin says Ukraine and Russia are one people. They call Ukraine 'Little Russia'. And you say this isn't an invasion or an occupation?

INDIA. That assumes the freedom-loving people of Ukraine would not welcome the overthrow / of a neo-Nazi junta –

ECHO. Oh, this is the people strewing flowers in the army's path?

VICTOR. Next / question –

ECHO. And really, honestly, how can you believe there is a neo-Nazi junta led by a Jew whose great grandfather was killed by Nazis and whose grandfather fought to liberate the country from the Germans?

INDIA. If the Zelenskys were not Nazis then / that doesn't mean –

YULIA *has re-entered. Surreptitiously, she is finding something on her phone.*

ECHO. A country is invaded, occupied and subjugated by a foreign power. The invasion is supported by collaborators. The invaders set up a puppet government under their control. But eventually the country will be liberated, but this time by its own people. Isn't that how the world will see it? Madam Acting President?

INDIA. You mean the Russians were the heroes then and they're the villains now?

ECHO. I'm just asking the question.

During this speech, YULIA *goes and shows images on her phone to* FOXTROT *and* ECHO.

INDIA. I was brought up to believe the Russians were unique. The mystic oneness of its people. The building of the first socialist state. Their courage in the face of Nazi terror, sacrificing untold millions to save the world from fascism. Now what are you saying? That Holy Mother Russia is just muddy villages and brutality and backwardness and vodka?

YULIA *holds the phone and its images up to* INDIA. VICTOR *quickly stands and goes to* YULIA.

VICTOR (*accusing, to* POLINA). A phone.

POLINA. I'm sorry, I…

YULIA. I took it back.

ECHO. What are…

YULIA. My schoolfriend. Instagram.

INDIA. Where is she?

YULIA. It's a little town, Kiev suburb really. Bucha.

POLINA. I am so sorry.

VICTOR *grabs her phone.* POLINA *takes* YULIA *by the arm and pulls her out of the room,* VICTOR *following.*

INDIA. She shouldn't have sent pictures. They can trace the phone.

FOXTROT. What did we see?

ECHO. Bodies. Civilian bodies, in the streets.

INDIA. A dead man by his garden gate.

ECHO. His dog…

FOXTROT. Of course, it might be… actors?

The landline rings. ECHO *quickly answers it.*

ECHO (*phone*). Victor.

I see. I understand. How's things at the airport?

And the convoy? Right.

Re-enter VICTOR, *holding Yulia's phone. He picks up the situation, but realises it's too late to stop what's happening.*

Any news about the junta? And the whereabouts? Oh, right. We'll set all that in train.

Of course.

He puts the phone down.

FOXTROT. So is this, are we the government?

ECHO. The Ukrainians bombed the runway at the airport. It was never possible to land troops there. The convoy's stuck in mud, literally. A sixty-kilometre traffic jam.

INDIA. And the junta?

ECHO. Zelensky made a selfie video on Friday. Clearly in Kiev, government building. With the cabinet. 'We're all still here.'

Slight pause.

We're not going to be the government.

The phone rings again. VICTOR *answers.*

VICTOR (*phone*). Hello, yes. Victor.

Did I?

Yes, of course, understood.

He puts down the phone.

They're sending vehicles to pick us up.

FOXTROT. To take us where?

INDIA. Where do you think.

ECHO. On the phone, they said there was a joke, by the Ukrainians. 'They used to say, Russia had the second best army in the world. Now it's the second best army in Ukraine.' I'll get my luggage.

(*To* VICTOR, *bitterly.*) 'All tongues, all cultures'. 'Democracy and freedom'.

He holds up his hand in a wave.

Do pobachennia Dnipropetrovsk. Do pobachennia Ukraine. [Goodbye Dnipropetrovsk. Goodbye Ukraine.]

He goes out.

FOXTROT. Will he need it?

VICTOR. What?

FOXTROT. His luggage.

VICTOR *doesn't reply.*

Not even Sport. I'll tell the others.

He goes out.

INDIA (*to* VICTOR). Well? 'Victor'?

VICTOR. Our aim was to liberate a grateful fellow-Slavic people from the yoke of the Americans. There was even talk of freedom and democracy. In just five days. But we've just found we can't win that war. So we'll just have to fight a war we can win. For something else.

INDIA. What's that?

VICTOR. Inch by inch. Smashed building by smashed building. Abandoned village by abandoned village. Dead soldier by dead soldier, dead child by dead child. The iron law of power, force and strength. Until one of us runs out.

He looks at INDIA.

It would have been you.

INDIA. And why the names?

VICTOR *holds up a splayed hand.* POLINA *enters.*

VICTOR. F for Foxtrot, I for India, V for Victor, E for Echo. Delta, Alpha, Yankee, Sierra.

INDIA. Ah.

He goes out.

POLINA. Um… is there anything…?

INDIA. Yes. Vodka.

THREE MATES

Natalka Vorozhbyt

translated by Sasha Dugdale

Character

ANDRIY

No… no… no… I'm not awake, I'm asleep… not fast asleep, but I'm definitely not awake, and I'll be asleep again in a moment for sure… I'll fall asleep and sleep like a baby until morning… It's happening… I'm dropping off now… I'm sleeping… and I'm dreaming, dreaming that… that I woke up. Whereas actually I'm… Shit. Fuck it, I'm awake. Shit shit shit. That's the second night. I've only had an hour and a half's sleep. I must have gone to sleep pretty quick, even dreamed a bit to begin with. But then it was as if my brain was switched back on. Maybe I was worrying about something… but now I've forgotten what it was. Yep, I can't remember what was worrying me, but I've woken up anyway. Well, that's it, I'm wide awake now. I've just got to not wake up Olga, she's a very light sleeper. I'll lie here and try to keep still. She'll kill me if I wake her up. Thing is, the harder you try to keep still the more you need to move. Gotta scratch my nose… and my big toe is itching… and my shoulder's gone numb, I need to sneeze, to fart, to turn over… I've had enough of this, maybe I should go and sleep on Vitaly's sofa. But the bed will squeak if I get up and that will wake her… okay, I'll just lie here and be patient – stare up at the new light. All those fancy glass bits I can't see in the total fucking darkness. I've got to get up early as well. I'm doing the morning service in church. It's like my hobby, I suppose, singing in the church choir at the weekends. Lying here, trying to empty my head of thoughts, but when you try not to think, the thoughts just keep on coming, intruding… Remembering all sorts of terrible shit, like when I wrapped a garlic clove in a sweet wrapper and gave it to my grandad and he spat and coughed for ages afterwards, or when Yarik and me put Tippex all over this girl Lesya's dress and shouted 'sperm! sperm!' all because we liked her and we were fuckwits back then… Oh! I've just remembered what woke me up. That stupid woman who conducts the choir wrote in the group chat that there was going to be an air raid tonight. Idiot woman. And I'm a fucking idiot, too. Every evening someone posts that there's going to be a rocket strike and I always fall for it. Why write those things?

Like, are you in intelligence or something? If there's an air raid then there's an air raid, we all get up and go wherever: the underground car park or the metro or the bathroom… whatever we've got used to… What's with the fucking prophet stuff?

Right, what's going on on socials. I'll turn on my side… gently does it… just so the phone light isn't directly in Olga's face. And of course, a message from Yarik in Vienna: 'Hey man, how are you doing? They say there's going to be a rocket strike tonight.' Another prophet. Fuck off, Yarik.

Sitting in Vienna and telling me when there's going to be a rocket strike. 'I'm worried,' he writes. (ANDRIY *speaks as he types*.) 'Don't you worry, you and your family are safe, that's the main thing, how are the kids? Are they asleep? Go back to sleep… it's not good for your health to get anxious…' They left and now they're fucking worried. And tomorrow they're off skiing in the Alps because it's the kids' holidays. (*Reads.*) 'I'm a bit nervous actually, haven't been skiing in years.' (ANDRIY *types*.) 'Yeah, it's totally terrifying, Yarik, maybe better not risk it…' And now he's taken offence.

He says: 'If everyone is killed in the war then who's going to continue the Ukrainian race?' Yarik, who the fuck needs people like you to continue the race, I mean, really…

Lord, how the hell am I going to get back to sleep now. Better if there *was* a rocket strike, at least it would justify my lack of sleep. I can spend the day with a face like a crumpled paper bag and no one will notice because everyone else looks the same.

The air raid siren sounds.

Oh. Look at that. Wish granted. That siren's gone off about a thousand times since the beginning of the fullscale invasion… and I've heard it every time. You think you might get used to it, but every fucking time the same feeling, like my stomach's dropping out of me, and there's a horrible metallic taste in my mouth. So we *are* going to have a fun night after all. For some reason Olga's still asleep, surprising because she's always the first to wake when the siren sounds. The boy's asleep as well, but he only wakes when there's an explosion. I won't wake them, I'll have a look, see what they're saying, what's flying where – and if anything's coming towards Kyiv I'll wake them. But let them sleep for a bit longer.

We've got a long hard winter ahead. Olga's got all anxious with these constant air raids. She's stopped waxing. She says she's too unwell with it all to go to her waxing. She just can't do it any more. I mean I couldn't care less about the waxing. She's the one with the weird obsession.

ANDRIY *reads Telegram:*

Okay, so what have we got:

Seven guided air missiles coming from Belgorod region.

Three drones from Kursk.

Six air-launched ballistic missiles from Tambov and up to twelve cruise missiles from the Caspian Sea.

They're heading for Kherson, Kharkiv, Sumy. For the moment, Kyiv is still on hold. I mean this is progress isn't it: you can be lying in your bed checking where from and at what speed ballistic missiles are flying in your direction… Where's my popcorn? You feel like a player in some great big lottery and you sure as hell don't want to win.

When I was a boy I never played war games, I don't much care about guns. I used to make mud pies with the girls – and now I could give a masterclass on ballistics, cruise missiles, rocket trajectories, to anybody – although who needs one? We're all experts here. I could give a lecture abroad but we aren't allowed to leave. That is, men aren't allowed to leave. Because I'm a male citizen of Ukraine and within the conscription age. Don't even ask how Yarik and the rest left. I wouldn't have done that. It was shameful. Dishonourable. But it's not just that I can't go abroad – I can't even go out on the streets of my own city, or take the metro or go to the supermarket or the cinema. I hardly go out the house at all. I buy all my food online. Because… they'd catch me. The ones who're already in are chasing all the other men of military age. They're carrying out raids, even. I mean, I work, I pay my taxes, I've never broken the law or committed an offence, I make regular donations to the army – but all the same they're out looking for me. I'm not complaining, it's all logical and that. They're hunting *me* down because Russia is hunting the lot of us down. And if we don't want to be hunted down, then we need to go to war and fight those fuckers. It's all justifiable and so on, I get it. But… like, it's crazy but, I don't *want* to join up. I'm in hiding. And you know why? Because if I *do* I could get killed… Well, I mean, I could get killed here as well, although the probability is far better here, I mean far lower. Some people are off fighting and others are hiding, and a third lot are hunting out the ones who are hiding, and a fourth lot have gone abroad, and another lot have got themselves an exemption from service…

At night I think about it and wonder how I fit in in all this. I'm no hero, that's for sure, but I'm not the bad guy either. I'm just an ordinary Kyivan boy. I like football, singing, my family. I really passionately love Kyiv, and my district, and when I look out the window at all those hideous new builds and my own native hills it gives me a hard-on, seriously. So if they tried to invade Kyiv I'd definitely fight them off. Although that's bullshit right there, because they already got pretty close. They got as far as the outskirts and I didn't do a fucking thing. I fled with my family to the west of Ukraine and stayed there three months until everything calmed down again. So what does that make me in all this? A coward? Yeah. A coward.

Although I'm less of a coward than Yarik, who paid a bribe of fifteen thousand dollars and escaped to Vienna. But then I'm more of a coward than Max who went and signed up on the very first day and has served two years now without rotation. He's a scout trooper. Max. He came back on leave once. He's changed… I can't really describe it in words… it's like the juice has been sucked out of him. Like he's been sucked dry. He looks like a stranger. Like he's come from another reality. Although actually… he has. Can you imagine it? We were all at the conservatoire together, same year. Me, Yarik and Max. We were mates, the three of us.

A loud explosion nearby.

Fucking hell, it's started. Olga'll kill me – I didn't wake her! How can she still be asleep? Olga! Hey, wake up! Quick, down to the car park!

*He shakes a pile of pillows in an attempt to wake it. He
suddenly remembers and stops in his tracks.*

Oh, I'm losing it… Yarik said we've all got some kind of PTSD,
only it comes out different in each of us. Must be this is *my*
version… They're in the UK. I took them to the station, day
before yesterday. They were both nervous wrecks, especially
after the latest attack and the hit on the block next to ours.
They applied for the refugee programme. And I thought she
was sleeping beside me, Olga… Fuck. I'm so glad you're in
the UK. The whole world is learning about Ukrainians through
our wives. Probably better that way as *wives* was always our
strong suit. I'm so glad you're in the UK. It's so shit you're in
the UK. I'm not going down to the underground car park on my
own. It was fun going together. Remember when you forgot to
put your pants on because you were so scared and you spent
the whole night like that, without them. Remember how we
laughed about it? And took all those naughty selfies and I went
down on you while the kid was sleeping in the other car? And
sometimes you made sandwiches and a hot thermos and we
had it very good. We drove down to the underground parking,
with our sandwiches and blankets, like we were out for a picnic.
An enforced picnic at night with the neighbours. One guy, this
hipster type with his own barber shop, he was conscript age, he
brought this see-through box, and it was filled with, like, little
biscuits, and I thought, oh, great, he's going to offer them round,
but then I looked closer and it's filled with snails… pet snails,
and he'd wrapped them in a blanket so they didn't get cold. Big
strong lad, military age, and he's keeping his pet snails warm.
Funny, right? I haven't seen him around for a while. Maybe he's
already gone to war… I mean, who brings a lot of snails to an
underground car park when there's an air raid? And one time
me and Olga were in a lighting shop and there was a daytime
air raid. We were looking for a little desk lamp for the kid –
and then right close to us there's a rocket strike. It's a big one,
powerful, smoke everywhere, explosions. And she went and
bought three chandeliers. Three fuck-off chandeliers with little
crystal bits everywhere. Later when we got home she admitted
that it'd been a moment of psychosis. We laughed about
that… And now I've got her psychosis hanging over my head,
twinkling away and reminding me… reminding me how nice it
was to go through all this fucking nightmare together.

The sound of explosions. ANDRIY *automatically ducks down as he listens.*

That's a Patriot! Anti-aircraft working hard! Well done, lads! Amazing anti-aircraft work! Yarik just posted on Facebook: how are you getting on there, Kyiv? Bastard, I so want to answer that post: 'How are you getting on there, Vienna? How about you, Munich?! Hey London and New York, how's things? Are you asleep!!!?'

ANDRIY *types.*

(*Proudly.*) I did it. I wrote: 'Fuck off, Yarik' right under his post where everyone can read it. I'm not putting up with his shit any more. What's next, you'll write to Max from the Alps to his trench near Avdiivka, ask him how Avdiivka's getting on? How's things in Bakhmut? The Alps are getting worried… Max hasn't been in contact for three days now. Three fucking days and nights. How are you, Max? Hey, how *are* you?! How are you… Are you still there? Hey, Max…!

Max is a mezzo-soprano. Get that? It's incredibly rare, there are only a few ever. He could sing in the best opera houses in the world. Max, not Yarik. Yarik's a very ordinary baritone. There are thousands like him. I'm a tenor, not that special either. Why him and not me? I already answered that question. Because I'm a coward. Olga's never going to be proud of me. Nor my son. He's already said that when he's old enough he wants to go and fight. He didn't say he was ashamed of me, but it was obvious. But then we'll be together for a long time. I'll watch him grow up, even if it is mostly on Zoom. I'll help him out, pay for his studies, his holidays, help him decorate his apartment, give him advice he doesn't want… I'll be useful to him in the future. If, that is, there is one… if no one suffers a heart attack or cancer or Russian occupation. And I won't care that they aren't proud of me, or that I haven't got a medal. I'll still have my arms and legs, won't I? And I can still have babies. I mean, if that's the right thing to be doing in a war… Like, as Yarik said, to continue the Ukrainian race… But does that mean that if Max is killed, then… No, that's total shit. More and more of the guys going to war now get their sperm frozen… Max, did you get your sperm frozen? Max? Who are you going to leave your country to? To a lot of cowards like us? If you want Olga to have your baby afterwards, you just say… Or Irka? Just make a list, it must get boring down in those trenches. We can put it out for tender. Sorry, sorry. You know my stupid jokes. Sorry, Olga. You, as well. You said you fell in love with my stupid sense of humour… and the great sex… Not my great courage.

ANDRIY *is now mainly addressing the pile of pillows:*

You'll say that Max was never a brave man – well, there's not much I can say back to that. He's just better than me. So why didn't you marry him, then? Because you're a pragmatist. Brave men aren't always the best for a family. Cowards are more afraid of losing, they cling on to life, and not to an idea. You like the good life, you like peace and quiet, you like to have some money in your pocket. You aren't worthy of him, of Max. You're worthy of me, a coward. But like all women you have fantasies of being the hero's widow. After all, you look pretty good in black. It suits you.

Well, forgive me for being such a loser and denying you that opportunity. But you try putting yourself in my place. You try it, Olga. You try it.

Would you go to war? There are mice there, Olga. Max wrote that he wakes up to mice nibbling his ear. They get into his clothes. They chew all the cables and devices. You could never get used to that. So you say back to me that thousands of women have signed up. It's true, I know. It's humiliating. I feel utterly destroyed by it. But they volunteer, right? If they want to fight, they fight, and if they don't want to, they don't. So then you say: it's not that they *want* to, it's just that they can't not go. Their conscience makes them go. Olga, you're fucking with me. If you want I'll go sign up tomorrow. You want that?! You'd get two hundred and your freedom. Find yourself some Brit… You can tell them what a hero I was… Why the hell am I getting at you like this? You've never once reproached me. Forgive me, Olga. Sometimes I make myself sick. Like right now. Like every night.

Max writes about the damp and the silence. About how animals seem to sense an attack coming… How they can't go and fetch the bodies of their friends from the battlefield and can only watch as they turn to compost… And every single one of them had been a whole universe, only the day before. When I read his posts it's like I'm reading fucking Remarque. Just a few hundred kilometres east of my warm bed my friend has just spent his sixth day in a trench. The batteries are all dead and he's wet through. His fingers and toes are frostbitten and his ration pack is gone. I just can't imagine it. I just can't.

And me, I faint at the sight of a fingernail being cut. Olga trims my nails and I have to shut my eyes. Don't believe me? It's true! Here, look!

He picks up nail scissors and cuts his nail, stares at it for some time and faints.

Still in a faint:

I am now unconscious… so I could say anything. I am a male Ukrainian citizen and I am thirty-six. I'm dodging conscription. I am nothing and nobody. My existence is shameful and worthless. Being a man is altogether shameful and worthless. Especially a Ukrainian man.

Some of us are draft dodgers, cowards running scared. Most of us just want to live. Even you in the trenches. Especially you in the trenches. You have a right to life. But us here, our life isn't worth fuck. Talking about men isn't, kind of, *done* right now. No one's writing about us, unless it's an obituary or screenplay about war heroes. If you're a man and you're not fighting then you're not allowed to have any kind of problem, you're not allowed to be poor or afraid or cheated on. You don't deserve to suffer.

Compared to the men fighting, the ones over there in the trenches, you're a pig in shit. Hard to imagine how many of us pigs in shit there are, hiding away in apartments, in towns and villages, depressed, utterly wretched…

There is one way of thinking about it: everyone will have to fight, everyone's hour will come, because this is going to be a long war. Thinking like that makes me feel calm, in a way, because… it's fate. I'm just waiting until I can't influence the outcome any more, until there's no choice.

Also they say that the EU only wants us because we're the one country in Europe that's got actual knowledge of fighting and can help push back Russia and the East, and definitely not because we are so amazing or because they really truly want to help us. They want our army with all its hard won skill to cover their own arses. Thank you for the honour of having to fight off Russia, thank you for entrusting us with this mission… But why us? What did we do? Who appointed us to this role? I'd complain but I don't know who to… Don't any of you want to take our place? Max's place? How about mine? Hey, I've warmed it up. It's still warm. Who of you wants to take my warm place?

The sound of an explosion, of many explosions. ANDRIY returns to consciousness. The sky is lit up as if by a huge firework display and the chandelier sways, casting fantastical shadows on the wall.

I wake up… and every time I wake I hope to God that the war was all just a bad dream. And I pray. But Lord, this isn't a dream. And once again I've got to choose: car park or bathroom? Conscription office or church choir? Action or shame? Life or death? Porridge or scrambled egg? Yarik, Max, me, we used to draw straws. But if the Russians, like, hit a power station and the electricity goes, I won't need a straw to work out that breakfast will be bread and butter. It's easier when there's no choice. When there's no choice left for any of us. Any one of us. But, for now, this is how we are…

ANDRIY begins singing an aria, perhaps 'Je crois entendre encore' from Bizet's Les pêcheurs de perles, *in harmony with the anti-aircraft guns. Every time a rocket or a Shahed drone is hit it's accompanied by a different sound and light effect. The chandelier swings ever more dramatically. Shrapnel from the rockets flies about, hitting buildings, now here and now there…*

The aria stops suddenly, and there is darkness.

WRETCHED THINGS

David Greig

For Nick Kent

*with grateful thanks for his endless enthusiasm,
determination, faith and patience in bringing these plays to life.*

'We men are wretched things, the gods have spun for us a life of
grief, while nothing troubles them.'

The Iliad, Bk 24

Characters

SASHA, *a Ukrainian Infantry soldier*
DIMYA, *a Ukrainian Infantry soldier*
SARGE, *a Ukrainian Infantry sergeant*
JIN, *a North Korean Infantry soldier*

Setting

An abandoned primary school, now in no man's land, somewhere on the frontline in Eastern Ukraine, sometime in the autumn of 2024.

The classroom is brutalised from shelling, abandonment, and having been shelter for soldiers over many months.

Windows have been shot out, rubble strewn across the floor, the detritus of war is everywhere.

A few children's pictures remain pinned to a wall. Small primary-school chairs and tables lie scattered about.

Some boxes of toys and a metal sink sit in the corner.

ACT ONE

Two soldiers enter, SASHA and DIMYA, both keep low, covering each other.

SASHA. Clear!

DIMYA. Clear!

SASHA. Clear!

DIMYA. Clear!

> *Satisfied, they slump exhausted. SASHA against a wall, DIMYA sitting on a little school chair. For a long time, they just try to get their breath back.*

SASHA. Sarge should be coming soon on the motorbike.

He can give us a ride back to Ikea.

DIMYA. Legs, arms, ears?

SASHA. Intact

DIMYA. I'm so tired.

SASHA. Hungry.

DIMYA. Did anyone see us come in?

SASHA. I don't think so.

DIMYA. They'll work it out eventually.

SASHA. Ten minutes. Fifteen.

We'll be back at Ikea by then.

DIMYA. Happy in the ballpit.

SASHA. Happy in the canteen.

> *Gunfire in the middle distance.*

> *SASHA brings his hands together, head slightly dipped.*

> *He closes his eyes.*

DIMYA. What are you doing?

SASHA. Listening for drones.

DIMYA. You're praying.

SASHA. So, what if I am?

DIMYA. I don't mind if you pray.

SASHA. I wouldn't care if you did mind.

DIMYA. You know what they say.

There's no atheists in a foxhole.

SASHA. You're an atheist.

DIMYA. I'm an agnostic. What are you praying for anyway?

SASHA. Just saying thank you.

DIMYA. For what?

SASHA. For us being alive.

DIMYA. I'd wait till we're home before thanking anyone
    for that.

SASHA. You said you weren't going to argue.

DIMYA. No, no, you carry on.

SASHA (*praying*). Dear Sweet Merciful Jesus, have mercy on
    a poor sinner, Sasha, a soldier fighting somewhere on the
    Eastern Front. I won't say where.

DIMYA. Why not?

SASHA. Op Sec.

DIMYA. With God?

SASHA. Whatever channel you're on, it's best to assume you
    can be overheard.

Thank you for keeping me alive.

My comrade Dimya is an agnostic so please accept my
thanks on his behalf. We still have two miles to go before
we reach our base in the old Ikea by the highway. In the
meantime, we give ourselves over to your keeping.

In the name of the Father, the Son and the Holy Spirit,
Amen.

DIMYA. Amen.

A moment.

Shit.

SASHA. What?

DIMYA. A dead Orc.

DIMYA *has seen* JIN.

SASHA. Still warm.

DIMYA. Must have been the one we shot on the way in.

SASHA. He's Korean.

DIMYA. He looks about twelve. Anything on him?

SASHA. ID tag, picture of his mother, Russian phrasebook.

DIMYA. 'Please', 'thank you', 'drop your weapon'.

SASHA. Cigarettes.

DIMYA *puts two cigarettes in his mouth.*

Lights them.

Coughs.

Gives one to SASHA.

DIMYA. What do they put in these things? Barn sweepings?

Both return to their places of rest, smoking.

SASHA. They treat the Koreans like shit.

DIMYA. They treat everybody like shit.

They smoke.

In the quiet of the moment, we hear a motorcycle.

It comes nearer.

SASHA. Sarge.

DIMYA. I wasn't sure he'd make it.

SASHA. Of course he made it. He's the best biker on the Eastern Front.

DIMYA. And he knows it.

The motorcycle arrives outside and stops.

ACT TWO

SARGE *enters. An older man.*

SARGE. Afternoon boys.

BOTH. Sarge.

SARGE. They told me you got into a spot of trouble.

DIMYA. Just a spot.

SASHA. We gave as good as we got.

DIMYA. There was an awful lot of them.

SASHA. They keep coming and coming.

DIMYA. It was like mowing grass.

SARGE. I see you've been busy with the fingerpaints?

SARGE *looks at the children's paintings.*

Long time since I was in primary.

DIMYA. Which Tsar was that under?

SARGE. Who's the stiff?

SASHA. Korean.

SARGE. Never seen one of them before.

SARGE *kneels by* JIN.

He's not dead.

SASHA. What?

SARGE. There's a pulse. Go into my pack. He needs water.

SASHA *goes to help* SARGE.

SARGE *puts* JIN *in a recovery position.*

Prepare to evacuate the casualty.

DIMYA. Sarge, there's only one bike.

SARGE. I'll take him. Then I'll come back for you two.

SASHA. Right.

DIMYA. Or?

SARGE. Or what?

DIMYA. You could take us first then come back for him.

SARGE. He'll die.

DIMYA. Which would be a shame but.

If he was Ukrainian –

SARGE. It makes no difference who he is.

DIMYA. It makes a bit of difference.

SARGE. We evacuate the wounded without distinction.

DIMYA. In ordinary circumstances, sure, but –

SARGE. No exceptions.

DIMYA. We're under fire.

SARGE. Don't patronise me, Private.

DIMYA. Sorry Sarge.

SARGE. We follow regulations, The Geneva Convention, and the International Laws of War: a wounded prisoner is treated humanely without distinction.

DIMYA. Yes but –

SARGE. What?

DIMYA. Rules have contexts.

If there's no space in the library, I park on a yellow.

Sasha fixes his neighbour's boiler cash-in-hand.

If you've got fifteen minutes before drones come in

You leave the dead guy.

SARGE. He's not a plumber any more, and you're not a librarian. You're private soldiers and you do what you're told.

BOTH. Yes Sarge. / Yes Sarge.

SARGE. Now, help me carry him out.

A big explosion nearby.

Jesus Christ!

They all drop down.

DIMYA. They're getting closer.

SARGE. I'll wait till they pass.

SASHA. Korean cigarette.

SARGE. Thank you.

SARGE *coughs.*

Goddamn what do they put in these things?

A moment.

DIMYA. The thing is Sarge –

SARGE. Not you again.

DIMYA. Actions have consequences.

That's the foundation of justice. And the Orcs,

I think they operate without moral standards.

You've seen the videos.

Hammers, graves, castrating prisoners,

bombed playgrounds, hospitals, schools.

Never a scrap of pity.

If we save him, all that wickedness has cost the Russians nothing.

SASHA. He's Korean.

DIMYA. They're worse.

SASHA. Are they?

DIMYA. You should read your history.

SARGE. It's not for me to judge, Dimya.

DIMYA. Personally, I'm happy to judge.

This man chose the wrong side of history. I think we should
leave him.

SARGE. Soldier, who are you fighting for?

DIMYA. Ukraine, Sarge.

SARGE. And what is Ukraine?

DIMYA. Ukraine is a proud and glorious land, an ancient tribe,
with broad-hipped mothers, and brave fathers, and plump,
rosy-cheeked children, Sarge.

SARGE. Ukraine is an idea.

At this moment, Ukraine is the idea that freedom can be
chosen.

And if we are to choose freedom, that means we must accept
the values that sustain that freedom.

The Geneva Convention, The Hague, the UN, the EU.

DIMYA. I don't mean to be cheeky, Sarge, but Sasha and
I have just survived a night and a day in the old Amazon
warehouse, up to our ankles in rats and water, under constant
fire with wave after wave of them coming at us… It was a
difficult shift, and I have to say, Sarge, over those long, dark
hours I have come to value life much more than I expected.
Suddenly simple things mean a great deal to me, things like
a tree, birdsong, Sasha breathing, and the blessed memory of
my first girlfriend's tits under her cashmere jumper.

SARGE. That's enough.

DIMYA. No.

I have not had enough, Sarge. Not nearly enough life. I can
feel it slipping from me in this bloody classroom and I want
to hold on. Every second we spend here is a roll of the dice.
I'm not prepared to stay a minute longer than we have to.

SASHA. Mate.

DIMYA. If a man is sliding down a roof, and he manages to grab on to the iron gutter with the fingertips of one hand, then four fingers, then three, then two, then one.

Finally, with his little finger, he still holds on.

Why?

SASHA. I don't know.

DIMYA. Nor do I.

But I do know one thing.

It isn't so his country can join the E fucking U.

SARGE. Son, you're young, I've seen this sort of thing before. It happens. You won't die. I'm a good biker. Best on the Eastern Front. The Orcs will never get me. I'll get out, zig zag, and get back here fast. You two just have to hold out a couple of hours more.

A huge window-shaking bomb nearby.

ALL. Shit! Damn! Fuck!

They are all thrown to the floor.

ACT THREE

Dust clears.

They rise again, carefully.

DIMYA. They're getting their eye in.

    From outside, distinctly, the noise of skylarks.

SASHA. Skylarks.

SARGE. They still sing.

DIMYA. You'd think they'd be distracted.

SASHA. They've got own thing going.

SARGE. Worms

    Disturbed by the bombs

    Upturned earth

    Like fields after ploughing.

DIMYA. How is he?

SARGE. Still breathing.

    A moment of mooching. Boredom.

    DIMYA explores. In the music cupboard he finds a xylophone. He plays the xylophone, maybe 'Für Elise'.

    SASHA looks at the children's paintings, hands behind his back, if he's in an art gallery.

SASHA. 'Road going into the distance'
Dimitri, age six
Beautiful.

    'My mummy'
Martina, age six
Very evocative.

'Crows on trees'
Volodymir, age five
Haunting.

'Icon'
Valentina, age seven
Our lord Jesus.

He looks around to see if there's anything else interesting.

I wonder what happened to the children who painted them.

SARGE. Probably dead, or in Siberia.

DIMYA *stops playing the xylophone.*

They deported the people here. That's what I heard anyway.

SASHA *looks under the sink. He undoes a valve and...*

A thin stream of water emerges...

He collects the water in children's cups.

SASHA *and* DIMYA *drink the water in small children's cups.*

DIMYA. God that's good.

SASHA. Heaven.

DIMYA. Feels like a five-star hotel in Dubai.

The two men bring over a child's cup of water and a damp rag. SARGE *uses it to clean* JIN*'s face.*

He rubs some water on his lips.

SASHA. The water's stopped.

The dripping water has run dry.

Not much left in the pipes.

Then a violent volley of fire and mortars.

DIMYA. Here come his mates.

SASHA. They've found us.

The three men fire back out of the broken windows.

Bullets crack and ping.

They fire back.

More fire.

They fire back.

SARGE. Stand back.

DIMYA *and* SASHA *stand back.*

SASHA *protects* JIN.

SARGE *throws a grenade.*

Boom.

He follows up with four swift clear shots – bang, bang, bang, bang: like picking cans off a wall.

Silence.

ACT FOUR

SARGE. Okay. Enough. I'm going to make a run for it.

Sasha, help me –

SARGE *moves* JIN, JIN *wails.*

DIMYA. Jesus Christ!

SASHA. He's in pain.

DIMYA. He's in pain. This is ridiculous. We have a chance to live. He has no chance. Let's just put him out of his misery. That's what I would want if I was him. Far away from home. I'd pray for the end. A cuddle and a bullet. That's what we'd do if he was a horse.

SARGE. Crucially, he's not a horse, he's a man and so he's subject to law.

DIMYA. I don't see any law here. Do you? Where is it? Over there in their filthy trenches?

In the Kremlin? In Washington? In Brussels? In Bakhmut? No. It's nowhere because it doesn't exist. There's no such thing as law except in our heads.

There's no law, only power. We have it. He doesn't.

Bang.

SARGE. If we abandon him, we must accept the abandonment of all prisoners, in any similar future circumstances.

DIMYA. I'd say these circumstances are pretty specific.

SARGE. Right is right whatever the circumstance.

DIMYA. What if right results in our own death?

SARGE. The consequence of a right action is not our concern.

DIMYA. I really think it is.

SASHA. Sarge – we need to move not talk.

We're not in the seminar room now.

We're on the Eastern Front.

SARGE. I'd say the Eastern Front of Ukraine is precisely the seminar room of the world right now.

SARGE *makes to pick up* JIN.

DIMYA. Wait –

SASHA. The sooner he goes the sooner he's back.

A moment.

DIMYA. I think you're forgetting Nietzsche.

SASHA. Who's Neitzsche?

SARGE. A Nazi.

DIMYA. He's not a Nazi, he's a much-misunderstood thinker.

SASHA. And would he get us moving? What would he say?

DIMYA. He'd say 'Lads, you're alive!

You touch, you want, you need,

you're filled with the urge to shape, to form to make:

Every beat of your heart floods you with the vast natural current of life which overwhelms everything…

Let life carry you.

Let life be your guiding star.'

SARGE. And what about honour.

DIMYA. Nobody cares about honour now, except thieves.

SARGE. Well, I do.

Because out there, in the dark woods, out of the sight of professors and poets and plumbers, in the dark places only soldiers go, the light that guides you home is honour.

And it guides us.

Honour doesn't care for time or place, or cause or pay, or politics or love or fear. It cares for your comrades, women and the fallen.

It's a light that means a soldier can look another soldier in the eye and say: 'I am your brother.'

I will not quench that light while I remain alive.

DIMYA. What a load of nonsense.

You could power a windmill with that speech.

SASHA. Look, Sarge, I'm not an egghead like Dimya, I'm not a warrior like you. I'm just a plumber, but the way I see it is this – when winter comes you fix the boiler or put a jumper on. You don't just sit and freeze.

Now, either you take this boy and we try to hold out till someone comes back, or else we shoot him now, and never tell anyone we found him alive.

A moment.

You're the commanding officer.

Which is it to be?

A moment.

A bang.

SARGE *is shot.*

He falls.

Dead.

Sarge.

DIMYA. Fucking hell.

SASHA. Sniper.

DIMYA. Shit.

SASHA. He was in front of the window.

DIMYA. Sarge.

SASHA. Talking

DIMYA. Sarge.

SASHA. Not concentrating.

Sniper over by the warehouses.

Sarge was standing by the window.

DIMYA. Fuck. Fuck. Fuck. Fuck.

ACT FIVE

DIMYA. You take the boy back on the bike.

I'll carry Sarge back on foot.

SASHA. How?

DIMYA. Through the drainage ditch behind the hedgerow.

SASHA. Don't be ridiculous. They're both dead. Let's just jump on the bike and go.

DIMYA. It's my fault he was talking. If I'd just done as I was told he'd be alive. Please. Let's follow his orders. You take the boy and I'll carry Sarge.

SASHA. I'm a plumber. I'm used to crawling through drains.

DIMYA. And I'm a writer. If I survive I'll only write another novel, and who wants that?

SASHA. Help me strap the boy onto my back.

They fix up an improvised sling to help DIMYA *carry* JIN.

DIMYA. Come on big fella.

Sasha's your Uber tonight.

Make sure and give him five stars if he gets you home.

No smoking, no hot food.

And no soiling the back seat please. Are you ready?

SASHA. Ready.

DIMYA. One second.

DIMYA *kneels before the child's picture of Jesus and whispers a prayer.*

In the name of the Father, the Son and the Holy Spirit.

BOTH. Amen. / Amen.

A moment.

SASHA. Are you sure that's Jesus?

DIMYA. Who else could it be?

SASHA. It looks like Harry Styles.

SASHA *lights a cigarette.*

DIMYA. Patron saint of librarians, it's well known.

SASHA. Cigarette?

DIMYA. Dear God, no.

Those things are pure Novichok. You go first.

SASHA. See you in Ikea.

SASHA *leaves with* JIN.

We hear the motorcycle start and drive away.

DIMYA *takes the picture of Jesus/Harry Styles. He folds it and puts it in his pocket. He picks up* SARGE *and puts him on his back.*

DIMYA *roars. He roars again.* DIMYA *leaves*

Volleys of artillery, sound of explosions, sound of mortars… it's brutal, continuous.

And then it stops. Skylarks.

TAKEN

Cat Goscovitch

Cast

ANNA, *Ukrainian. Mother. Thirties*

LILYA, *Ukrainian. Anna's daughter. Twelve*

RUSSIAN SOLDIER, *twenties*

OLENA, *Ukrainian. Human rights lawyer for a children's charity. Thirties*

DMITRY, *Russian. Youth worker in a re-education camp. Twenties*

TV PRESENTER AND CAMERA PERSON, *Russian. Thirties*

Scene One

A living room in Mariupol.

Most of one wall is missing. The furniture is covered in debris, dust and splinters of glass. A wardrobe is pushed up against the window.

ANNA walks on stage, wearing a woollen hat, an anorak, and holding a small cake. She stops, stands very still, and starts to cry.

A moment.

She walks over to the dining table, brushes debris off a corner, covers it with a napkin, and puts the cake on top.

LILYA (*offstage*). Mum?

> *ANNA abruptly stops crying. Wipes her tears with the back of her hand.*

ANNA (*brightly*). One moment.

> *ANNA takes a candle from her pocket, sticks it in the cake and lights it.*

(*Brightly.*) You can come in now.

LILYA walks on stage. She wears an anorak and a scarf.

(*Singing.*)
Happy birthday to you,
Happy birthday to you –

LILYA. – Oh my God! Medovyk!

ANNA (*singing*).
Happy birthday, dear Lilya,
Happy birthday to you.

LILYA. It's amazing.

ANNA. I have no idea what it'll taste like… I had no eggs or sour cream, and it's just buckwheat flour, but Nica gave me some honey and –

LILYA. – Can't believe you managed to bake –

ANNA. – Steam.

We hear shelling in the distance.

Pretend there's twelve candles.

ANNA *pulls her phone out of her pocket.*

I promised your dad a video.

ANNA *videos* LILYA.

LILYA (*to the camera*). I love you Dad.

ANNA. Make a wish.

LILYA *closes her eyes, makes a heartfelt wish and blows out the candle.*

And a photo… smile.

LILYA *doesn't smile.*

LILYA. Do you think the war will be over when I'm thirteen?

A shell lands nearby.

ANNA *puts her phone in her pocket.*

ANNA. That was close.

LILYA. Is it bad that I no longer notice the shelling?

ANNA. They usually stop for breakfast.

ANNA *hands* LILYA *a present.*

I wanted to get you some new clothes but –

LILYA *unwraps the birthday present.*

LILYA. Shower gel?

ANNA. For when we have a shower again.

LILYA *smells it.*

LILYA. Smells of Dad. Can we call him?

ANNA. Nica says there's a store on Pashkovskoho Street that has a generator… We can go there when the shelling stops… hopefully we can catch the internet and charge our phones.

LILYA. Can missing someone hurt your body? Can it kill you? Like a bomb or a gun?

The shelling intensifies. ANNA *looks towards the window.*

ANNA. I'm sorry, sweetie… We need to go back to the basement.

LILYA*'s face drops.*

LILYA. Can we stay for just like one more minute? Please.

ANNA. One more minute.

A sad beat.

(*Brightly.*) Let's play pretend.

LILYA (*unenthusiastic*). You go first.

ANNA. Okay… We're going to the mall to get you some new clothes. And then, your friends are coming here for a birthday party.

LILYA. Is Tatiana coming?

ANNA. She's coming early to help you decorate the room.

LILYA. Is she bringing her new kitten?

ANNA. She's tucking it into her jacket to keep it warm… She wants you to help her name it.

LILYA. Is it bad that Tatiana was killed and I wasn't? Like if there was a trade-off –

ANNA. – We don't trade lives.

LILYA. If God said to me, Tatiana can live but you have to die.

ANNA. God would never do that. He loves all his children. Don't talk like that. It's your birthday.

ANNA *plays a K-pop song on her phone.*

Let's be HAPPY!

LILYA *smiles.*

They do a K-pop dance together. They're focused. In synchronicity for a few moves and then it falls apart.

LILYA. No, Mum… you're doing it all wrong.

ANNA. Am I?

LILYA. Look.

LILYA *stops the music and shows* ANNA.

You step across and then you do the arms.

ANNA *copies.*

ANNA. Like this?

LILYA. No! Opposite arms to legs… Oh my God.

LILYA *shows her again, taking this very seriously.* ANNA *copies.*

Yes.

ANNA. Okay, got it.

LILYA. Finally.

ANNA *starts the music again and turns up the volume.*

They dance in synchronicity for longer this time, then it falls apart, but this time ANNA *continues to dance.*

LILYA *stops dancing and laughs.*

And now ANNA*'s hamming it. Exaggerating the dance moves to amuse* LILYA. *Anything to distract her from the war.*

A RUSSIAN SOLDIER *walks through the hole in the wall. The sound of his radio and footsteps drowned out by the shelling and the music.*

His uniform is new, his face is covered. He carries an AK12 rifle and has a Z patch on his arm. LILYA *sees him but* ANNA *doesn't.*

Mum!

ANNA *continues to dance. Guessing at the words and singing along.*

MUM!

LILYA *rushes over and turns off the music.* ANNA *turns and is surprised to see the* SOLDIER.

SOLDIER. Documents.

ANNA *is out of breath from dancing.*

She opens her anorak and pulls out a zip-locked bag hanging around her neck, takes out two Ukrainian passports and hands them to the SOLDIER.

Your daughter shouldn't be here.

ANNA. We just came upstairs to get something… I'm taking her back to the basement.

SOLDIER. We're evacuating all the children from Mariupol.

ANNA. Let's go downstairs, Lilya. Get your cake.

SOLDIER. They're being taken to a holiday camp across the border in Crimea to give them a vacation from the shelling.

LILYA. Polina went there last week.

ANNA. Why didn't you tell me?

LILYA. I thought you knew… She sent me a video. She was playing in a playground. She looked happy.

ANNA. You're not going, Lilya.

The sound of a warplane.

SOLDIER. It's just for two weeks, and then we'll bring her back.

LILYA. Nothing bad happened to Polina, so why would it happen to me?

ANNA (*to* LILYA). I said no.

The SOLDIER *gives* ANNA *her passport.*

What about my daughter's passport?

SOLDIER. She needs to come with me.

ANNA. Please give me my daughter's passport back.

SOLDIER. If she doesn't come with me now, she'll be taken by force later.

ANNA. I want my daughter's passport.

SOLDIER. There's a bus about to leave. There's lots of other children on it. She'll be safe… Don't you want your daughter to be safe?

LILYA. It's okay.

LILYA *hugs* ANNA.

I love you, Mum. Charge your phone, catch the internet… I'll spam-message you when I get there… and you have to promise to read every one of them.

ANNA. But Lilya, I –

The SOLDIER *leads* LILYA *off the stage and through the auditorium.*

The lights fade.

Scene Two

An office in Kyiv.

Pot plants.

Wooden Scandinavian furniture.

An Apple laptop is on a table with two chairs in front.

A traumatised ANNA, *still wearing her anorak, a bag strapped across her body, stands in the centre of the room.*

OLENA *makes coffee.*

OLENA. It's not your fault.

ANNA. I made the decision. No one else. I should have insisted –

OLENA. – What happened to your daughter is a war crime… No one's allowed to steal children.

ANNA. They can't steal them unless they find them.

OLENA *pours the coffee.*

He said he'd bring her back in two weeks. In two weeks, she's going to be thirteen… My husband said I should have hidden her, but where? Where could I have hidden her? The next day, the soldiers came to our basement and took the rest of the children… even the babies.

OLENA *puts two cups of coffee on the table.*

Do you know where she is?

OLENA *pulls out a chair and gestures for* ANNA *to sit.*

OLENA. She won't be in Crimea now. That's a filtration camp.

ANNA *and* OLENA *sit next to each other.* OLENA *opens her laptop.*

We ran the photo you gave us through a facial recognition programme, and found several matches that could be your daughter.

OLENA *clicks the mouse.*

Why don't we start with the adoption listings.

ANNA *turns the laptop towards* ANNA.

This is a Ukrainian girl who was abducted and is now listed for adoption in Russia. Is she your daughter?

ANNA *looks at the photo.*

ANNA. No.

OLENA. Are you sure? It's been nearly a year since you saw Lilya. Girls change a lot at that age.

ANNA. I'm sure.

OLENA *clicks the mouse.*

OLENA. This was taken in a classroom in one of the re-education camps… girl at the desk in the middle, next to the window.

ANNA. She looks a bit like her but she's not my daughter.

OLENA *clicks the mouse.*

OLENA. This next one is a video. It's hard to watch.

The video plays. We hear military music.

ANNA. What are they doing?

OLENA. They force our children to take part in military training… Girl next to the boy in camouflage.

A beat.

ANNA. That's her. That's Lilya.

OLENA. You sure?

ANNA *leans into the laptop.*

ANNA. Play it again.

OLENA *plays the video again.*

Look at her little face. She hates it… Lilya would hate that.

OLENA. This was filmed a week ago and posted on Telegram. Our team managed to locate it in Secondary School No. 26… It's an hour from Moscow by train.

ANNA. Polina's mum said I have to get her myself.

OLENA. I'm sorry, I have no legal tools to return your daughter to you… Putin doesn't listen to the law.

ANNA. Of course, I'll go.

OLENA. You can't fly to Russia directly. They wouldn't let you in.

OLENA *hands* ANNA *a train ticket and some money.*

You take the train. Kyiv to Warsaw. This is Polish złoty to buy a ticket from Warsaw to Minsk. Journey time: twenty hours… there's an open border in Belarus. You'll be stopped and interrogated.

ANNA. Polina's mum said they held her there for three days.

OLENA. I hope it won't be so long for you… you mustn't tell them your husband's fighting on the front. And don't tell them you want to bring your daughter back to Ukraine. If it gets too much, ask for some water. It gives you time.

OLENA *places a bottle of pills on the table.*

You'll be tired. You'll be stressed. You'll need these.

ANNA. What are they?

OLENA. Tranquillisers.

ANNA. No, I –

OLENA. – Take them. The most important thing is to stay calm. The less emotion you show, the better. You don't care. You're as casual as if you're crossing the border to shop for bread.

OLENA *places a phone on the table.*

This is your burner phone. Leave your real phone in Ukraine. Memorise my number. It mustn't be on this phone… Call me anytime. Day or night. I'll help you in any way I can.

ANNA *puts everything in her bag.*

I'm sorry you have to do this alone.

OLENA *holds out the cup of coffee.*

Drink. The coffee's good here. You'll feel better.

ANNA *takes it and drinks.*

Every child that comes back is proof that Russia is committing a war crime. Every child that comes back is a gift from God.

The lights slowly fade.

Scene Three

Secondary School No.26 in Moscow Oblast.

Institutionally bright.

The faint, echoey sound of the Russian anthem being sung by children. It comes from behind a door and down a corridor.

ANNA, *wearing a long coat, her bag strapped across her body, carries a shopping bag.*

She stands centre stage.

ANNA. O Lord, please give my daughter back to me,
for Thy name's sake. Lord, have mercy. Holy God, Holy
Mighty, Holy Immortal, have mercy on us.

> *Lights up on an unassuming slouchy 'youth worker'.*
> *He stands in the auditorium wearing a black tracksuit with*
> *a Russian flag patch on his sleeve.*

> ANNA *peers into the auditorium.*

DMITRY. God is preparing a great victory for Russia.

> DMITRY *walks towards the stage.*

How did you get here?

> *He steps onto the stage and stands across from* ANNA.

ANNA. Do you have some water?

> DMITRY *looks at* ANNA *for a beat then walks offstage.*

> ANNA *is close to a panic attack. She takes deep breaths to try to calm herself.*

DMITRY (*offstage*). No one of that name is here.

> DMITRY *walks back on stage.*

> ANNA *collects herself.*

ANNA. Have they taken her somewhere else?

DMITRY. She was never here so how could she be taken
somewhere else?

> DMITRY *hands* ANNA *a bottle of water.*

You claim to be her mother.

ANNA *drinks the whole bottle in one go.*

ANNA. I am her mother.

DMITRY. Even if –

ANNA *opens her bag and takes out a file.*

ANNA. – I have the paperwork, her birth certificate.

DMITRY. We don't accept Ukrainian documents. They have to be in Russian.

ANNA. She was born in Ukraine. Why would they be in Russian?

DMITRY. We shouldn't be thinking about formalities here… We need to think about the best interest of the child.

ANNA. I don't have her passport… the soldier took it, do you –

DMITRY. – The special military operation is over for Lilya. Why would you want her to go back?

ANNA. I have no intention of taking my daughter back to Ukraine. I'm just here for a short visit and then I'll go back alone.

DMITRY. You have to think about her future. She has everything she needs here.

ANNA. I'm not here for her future. I'm here for today. Just for today… It's been nearly a year… I…

A beat.

I want to see her face.

DMITRY. Wait.

DMITRY *walks offstage.*

ANNA (*calling after him*). Where are you going? Are you bringing her to me?

From the assembly, we hear the children shout: Slava Rossii!

(*Whispers.*) Slava Ukraini.

ANNA *makes the sign of the cross.*

She takes out the bottle of tranquillisers from her bag, throws a pill down her throat.

The sound of a bell and a class changeover. Children's footsteps, muted conversation.

A long moment. ANNA *waits. Agitated.*

LILYA *appears in the auditorium. She wears a green military uniform with a Russian flag patch on the sleeve. Her hair tied back in a ponytail.*

LILYA. Mum?

ANNA *peers into the blackness of the auditorium.*

ANNA. Lilya?

LILYA. Oh my God, Mum!

LILYA *rushes onto the stage and they hug.*

ANNA. Lilya!

ANNA *is so overjoyed to see* LILYA *that she lifts her off her feet and plants kisses all over her face.*

You've grown so much… You're nearly as tall as me.

LILYA. I can't believe it. You're here. You're really here.

LILYA *laughs.*

This isn't pretending?

LILYA *'s face drops.*

I'm sorry about Dad.

ANNA. He can't wait to see you.

LILYA *looks confused.*

LILYA. He's alive?

ANNA. Of course. Thank God.

LILYA *pinches* ANNA.

Ow. What are you doing?

LILYA. Making sure you're real.

ANNA *hugs* LILYA.

ANNA. I've missed you so much.

LILYA *breaks the hug.*

LILYA. They said I can see you for ten minutes then I have to go back to class.

ANNA *puts her hands on* LILYA*'s face.*

ANNA. No, Lilya… you're not going back to class. I'm taking you home.

LILYA. To Mariupol?

ANNA. I've rented an apartment in Kyiv. Polina's in the same block.

LILYA. Polina's in Ukraine?

ANNA. Her mother came to get her like I've come to get you.

The bell goes.

LILYA *steps away from* ANNA.

LILYA. They don't like us to be late.

ANNA. There's no class any more, Lilya. I'm taking you home.

LILYA. They won't let you. You'll leave and I'll stay.

ANNA. They have to. I'm your mother.

LILYA. Not any more.

ANNA. Of course I am.

LILYA. They've given me a new mum.

ANNA*'s face drops.*

I'm moving in with her next week. I have my own bedroom. She let me choose the furniture. And when you open the cupboard, there's lights… she's getting me a kitten.

ANNA. They can't do that.

LILYA. It's Russian law… once I've been here a year, I have to have a new mum.

ANNA. No, they –

ANNA *bends over her bag to hide her emotions. She collects herself and takes out a piece of –*

LILYA. Medovyk?

ANNA. Got a bit squashed on the journey… It's light on the sour cream but this time I made it with flour and eggs.

ANNA *holds it out and* LILYA *takes a bite.*

LILYA. Is it bad that I dream of eating Medovyk?

ANNA. You can eat the rest of it on the train back home.

ANNA *wraps it back up. Holds out a plastic bag.*

These are the birthday clothes I wanted to get you last year.

LILYA *doesn't take them.*

Get out of that horrible uniform.

LILYA *points at a CCTV camera.*

LILYA. There's cameras. They're everywhere.

ANNA *glances at the cameras. She takes off her coat and holds it up.*

ANNA. Get changed behind this.

LILYA *hesitates.*

Come on, Lilya. I can't bear to see you in that for a minute longer. If your dad saw you like that.

LILYA *takes the bag and goes behind* ANNA *'s coat to get changed.*

We've done nothing wrong. They make us feel like it's our fault. Like we're wrong and they're right. The woman who helped me find you, Olena, she's a lawyer, she told me… It's not our fault. It's Putin. He's going to be arrested for what he's done to you. They're going to put him in jail… He can't go around stealing children… He's like the wickedest of goblins –

LILYA *steps out from behind the coat in her birthday clothes.*

They fit you perfectly.

LILYA. Jeans are a bit loose.

ANNA. You'll grow into them.

LILYA. I like things to be tight.

ANNA *hugs* LILYA. DMITRY *stands in the auditorium.*

DMITRY. What a beautiful reunion. Warms the heart.

He turns to the camera person.

Did you get that?

ANNA *holds* LILYA*'s hand.*

DMITRY *walks through the auditorium and onto the stage. He's followed by a camera person and a* TV PRESENTER.

We just need to do a little interview and then you're free to go.

ANNA. You're not going to try to stop me from taking Lilya back to Ukraine?

DMITRY. We would never stop a mother from being reunited with her daughter. Who do you think we are? Monsters?

ANNA *looks uncertain.*

All three of them step onto the stage.

The PRESENTER *hands* ANNA *a bouquet.* ANNA *looks bewildered. The* PRESENTER *hands* LILYA *a colourful teddy bear and an iPhone.*

LILYA *is used to this bizarre behaviour and takes it in her stride.*

LILYA. Thank you.

DMITRY *takes a photo with his phone.*

PRESENTER. Lilya, tell us, how was your time at the holiday camp?

LILYA *glances at* DMITRY.

LILYA. Good.

PRESENTER. How was the food?

LILYA. Lavish. We had meat every day and fruit.

PRESENTER. You're Lilya's mother. And you've come to take Lilya back to Ukraine.

ANNA. Yes

PRESENTER. Do you have a message for the Russian people?

ANNA. I –

DMITRY *walks over and talks quietly to* ANNA. *He stays standing next to her but out of shot of the camera.*

I want to say thank you to the Russian people for being so big-hearted and looking after my daughter.

ANNA *glances at* DMITRY.

I would say to any mother in Ukraine, there's nothing to worry about, you're welcome to come and pick up your child and bring them back to Ukraine.

The PRESENTER *turns to* DMITRY.

PRESENTER. You're one of the youth workers here.

DMITRY. Yes.

PRESENTER. Russia faces allegations of unlawfully taking and holding these children against their will. What is your response?

ANNA *and* LILYA *hug.*

DMITRY. Here, a mother is reunited with her daughter and free to take her home. Russia has done nothing but provide care and protection.

Black.

Scene Four

The train to Kyiv – carriage

LILYA sits, glued to her phone. A few seconds of a Russian song – swipe – a few seconds of Russian dialogue – swipe – a Russian song.

ANNA stands in the aisle drinking a take-out coffee. She holds out a bottle of water for LILYA.

ANNA. Water?

> *LILYA doesn't respond.*

> Why don't you come off your phone for a bit?

> *ANNA places it on the seat next to her.*

LILYA. You want me to not have a social life?

ANNA. I thought we could talk.

LILYA. Why would I want to do that?

ANNA. In ten minutes, we're going to arrive in Yahodyn and your dad's going to call… We need to work out what we're going to say to him… And we don't speak Russian any more.

> *LILYA looks up from her phone.*

LILYA. Oh my God, in Russia, I wasn't allowed to speak Ukrainian, and in Ukraine, I'm not allowed to speak Russian?

ANNA. We're allowed to speak it. But we choose not to.

> *LILYA rolls her eyes.*

> Your dad isn't fighting for himself. He's fighting for your future.

> *LILYA puts her phone down.*

LILYA. What gun does he use?

ANNA. How would I know?

> *ANNA finishes her coffee and crumples the cup.*

LILYA. I'm guessing it's an AK-74. We had the newer Kalashnikovs in our school, the AK-12s and the AK-15s.

ANNA. What?

LILYA. I can disassemble a Kalashnikov assault rifle in twenty-five seconds, clean run… I'm going to ask Dad what his fastest time is.

ANNA. They gave you a gun?

LILYA. I bet I can beat him. Children are quicker because our hands are smaller.

ANNA. They gave you a gun?

LILYA. I liked it.

ANNA. You don't know what you like. You don't know what you're talking about.

LILYA *glares at* ANNA.

LILYA. Stop treating me like I'm a child.

ANNA. What have they done to you?

LILYA. What have they done to me? What have you done to me? The Special Operation was over, and you bring –

ANNA. – It's called a war.

LILYA. You should never have come to get me then you and Dad could have had some nice little memory of Lilya, because all you have is me now, and you hate me, don't you?

ANNA. I love you.

LILYA. You're lying.

ANNA. I could never hate you.

LILYA. There was this girl in our class. She was from Mariupol. She was shot by a sniper. And when the doctor took the bullet out of her arm, it was an American cartridge, not a Russian one… You told me it was the Russians who were bombing us.

ANNA. You were there. Has Russia taken out your eyes?

LILYA. You insisted I go to Crimea.

ANNA. *I* insisted?

LILYA. You said Polina would be there.

ANNA. Sweetie, I –

LILYA. – She wasn't.

A beat.

You said, I'll be there for two weeks, and then I'll come home.

ANNA. The soldier said –

LILYA. – I waited for you, but you never came.

ANNA. I couldn't… you know I couldn't. Mariupol was under siege.

LILYA. They told me you'd abandoned me. They said my dad had been killed at the front, and I had to think about my future.

ANNA. They said that?

LILYA. I put you and Dad behind a wall. Told myself to never think about Ukraine again or I'll go crazy… The teachers were horrible. The soldiers would fire in the air to frighten us… I kept thinking, there's another universe, and in that universe, there's no war, and I live there with you and Dad…

ANNA. I found one driver who offered to smuggle me out. He wanted eight thousand US dollars, not Hryvnia –

LILYA. – Things get worse. They don't get better. That's what life is now.

ANNA. Remember the pigeons? They were always on our balcony… And then one day, they were gone. We should have left with the pigeons. I should have listened to your dad. He told us to leave but I was scared.

LILYA. Well you weren't wrong, were you… Look what happened to Tatiana.

LILYA starts to cry.

As soon as I'm sixteen, I'm going back to Russia. Matvey said they'll give us money and an apartment.

ANNA. Matvey? Who's Matvey?

LILYA. My boyfriend.

ANNA. Lilya, you're twelve years old.

LILYA. In two days, I'm going to be thirteen.

ANNA. And that makes you old enough to have a boyfriend?

LILYA. Was I old enough to have my best friend killed? Was
I old enough to see dead bodies on the street?

ANNA. That was different.

LILYA. Different how?

ANNA. How old is he?

LILYA. Fifteen.

ANNA. Lilya, no.

LILYA. He was the only person who was nice to me. The only
person who talked to me. Everything's confusing and when
I'm with Matvey it's not.

ANNA *'s phone rings.*

ANNA. That's your dad.

ANNA *takes her phone out of her bag.*

He wants to talk to you – don't tell him about the – just –
let's be happy.

LILYA Happy?

ANNA. We're having a family reunion. This is a happy
moment.

LILYA. Like my birthday?

ANNA *holds out the phone to* LILYA.

ANNA. Answer it.

LILYA *doesn't take the phone.*

Lilya, answer.

LILYA. But I don't remember him… I don't remember what he
looks like.

ANNA. For God's sake, answer. ANSWER.

LILYA *takes the phone.*

Attempts to look like she hasn't been crying. Holds the phone in front of her.

Prepares a smile.

Answers.

LILYA. Dad?

Black.

End.

116

Biographies

JONATHAN MYERSON

Jonathan Myerson is an Oscar-nominated and BAFTA-winning writer and director. His most recent work is *Nazis: The Road to Power* and *Nuremberg*, both 16-part scripted podcasts for BBC Sounds. *The Canterbury Tales* (HBO/S4C) was his first animated film – as writer-director, he was nominated for an Oscar and won a BAFTA, four primetime Emmys and other awards worldwide. He has written over forty original plays for audio and created the series *Number 10* for BBC Radio 4 which won the 2010 Writers Guild Award for Best Radio Drama, and many adaptations, including *Vasili Grossman's Life and Fate*, a modernised version of Trollope's *The Way We Live Now* and a dramatisation of Hogarth's *A Harlot's Progress* and *Marriage À La Mode*. He is the author of two novels – *Noise* and *Your Father* – both published by Headline Review. He wrote a column in the *Guardian* about his experiences as a local councillor in Lambeth, and for ten years he ran the MA in Creative Writing at City University London.

DAVID EDGAR

David Edgar's original plays for the Royal Shakespeare Company include *Destiny* (1976), *Maydays* (1983, Plays and Players Best Play Award), *Pentecost* (1994, Evening Standard Best Play Award) and *The New Real* (2024). His work for the National Theatre includes *Entertaining Strangers* (1987), *The Shape of the Table* (1990), *Albert Speer* (2000) and *Playing with Fire* (2005). His adaptations include a multi-award-winning version of Dickens' *Nicholas Nickleby* (RSC, 1980-1) and *A Christmas Carol* (2017-22). His other recent work includes *A Time to Keep* (with Stephanie Dale, Dorchester Community Play, 2007), *Black Tulips* (for *The Great Game*, 2009), *If Only* (Chichester Festival Theatre, 2013), and *Here in America* (Orange Tree, Richmond, 2024). In 2018 he wrote and presented a touring solo show, *Trying It On*. His book about playwriting, *How Plays Work*, was published by Nick Hern Books in 2009, and *The Little Black Book of the Populist Right* (with Jon Bloomfield, Byline Books) in 2024.

DAVID GREIG

David Greig is a writer and theatre director, born in Edinburgh in 1969. His first play *Europe* was performed at the Traverse Theatre in 1994. Since then, his plays, adaptations and musical theatre scripts have been performed widely in the UK and around the world. David has collaborated with Nick Kent on a number of his portmanteau projects, including *Miniskirts of Kabul* about Afghanistan, *Letter of Last Resort* about nuclear weapons, and *The Kid* about drones. In 2016 he became the Artistic Director of The Edinburgh's Royal Lyceum Theatre which he ran until 2024. In 2023 he published his first novel, *Columba's Bones*.

NATALKA VOROZHBYT

Born in Kyiv in 1975, Natalka is a playwright, screenwriter, film director and curator of social theatre projects. She has written more than fifteen plays, which have been translated into fourteen languages and performed all over the world – including at the Royal Court Theatre and the Royal Shakespeare Company in the UK, and Münchner Kammerspiele in Germany. Her plays include *Bad Roads* (for which she was named a laureate of the Taras Shevchenko National Prize of Ukraine in 2022); *The Grain Store*; *Maidan: Voices from the Uprising*; *Take the Rubbish Out, Sasha*; *Green Corridors*; and *Non-existent*. Natalka's award-winning work for screen includes adapting and directing *Bad Roads* for film in 2020, the 2022 short film *Are You OK?*, and her 2024 film *Demons*. She also wrote and executive produced the Ukrainian TV series *To Catch the Kaidash*, which won the Golden Dzyga Award for the Best TV Series 2021. In 2020 Natalka received the Women in Arts Award for her contribution to the film and theatre industries and in 2021 she received the Oleksandr Dovzhenko State Prize of Ukraine for outstanding contribution to the development of Ukrainian cinema. Natalka's work often explores themes related to life in her home country of Ukraine.

SASHA DUGDALE

Sasha Dugdale is a poet and translator. Her sixth collection *The Strongbox* (Carcanet, 2024) won the Runciman Award and was shortlisted for the London Hellenic Prize. In 2016 she won a Forward Prize for her monologue in the voice of Catherine Blake, the widow of William Blake, and she has been shortlisted for both the T. S. Eliot and Derek Walcott Prizes. As a translator she works primarily with women's voices. She has translated Ukrainian playwright Natalka Vorozhbyt for over twenty years, and her translation of Vorozhbyt's *The Grainstore*, set during the Ukrainian Holodomor, was staged by the Royal Shakespeare Company in 2009. Her translation of *Bad Roads*, Vorozhbyt's play about the war in Donbas, was commissioned and staged by the Royal Court Theatre. Dugdale's translations of exiled Russian poet Maria Stepanova have been shortlisted for the International Booker Prize and PEN Translates Awards, among others.

CAT GOSCOVITCH

Cat Goscovitch is the writer of the independent feature film *The Turtle and the Sea* (2016), which won Best Local Picture at the Birmingham Film Festival and is available on Amazon Prime. She also wrote the play *A Russian Doll* (2021), directed by Nicolas Kent, which premiered at The Barn. She is currently writing *Giant*, a TV series inspired by her experience in the music industry when she was signed to Sony as a singer.